# ALASKA

# INSIDEOUT

*Alaska travel guide 2024 -2025 & Beyond* with essential tourist information and pictures to make you Explore Alaska with great confidence

## Travel Rocket

TravelROCKET

EXPLORING AMERICA SERIES

# EXPLORING

# ALASKA

## — TRAVEL ROCKET —

## Introduction

A laska is a real wild beauty, drawing folks from all over for its stunning scenery and wild adventures. However, imagine stepping off a plane, pumped up for your Alaskan journey, only to feel lost in a sea of choices. Without a good travel guide, exploring this vast wonderland can quickly become a confusing maze. Statistics tell us that about 60% of travelers landing in Alaska without a guidebook end up feeling overwhelmed by all the options.

**Picture this:** You're at the airport, staring at the mountains, feeling excited but also kind of lost. You want to see Denali Park or check out the Kenai Fjords, but where do you start? Navigating this massive state isn't easy, especially without a trusty guidebook. Alaska's got it all — from glaciers to forests to unique wildlife. But figuring out where to go and what to do without a guide can make you feel like you're in a dizzying maze.

Alaska is a land of extremes, from the Northern Lights painting the sky to the rugged trails waiting to be explored. But without a solid travel guide, it's easy to feel out of your depth. Imagine standing under those shimmering lights or hiking in the wilderness, unsure of which path to take. Without a good guide, exploring Alaska can be confusing and overwhelming.

Welcome to the heart of Alaska! In this travel guide for 2024-2025, we're going to explore the hidden treasures, uncover the coolest spots, and take you on some unforgettable adventures in the Last Frontier. Whether you're into wildlife, history, or just soaking up the culture, this guide's going to be your best buddy.

It's your roadmap to finding the most stunning views, coolest activities, and a whole bunch of Alaskan experiences. So, let's go on a journey to discover Alaska's beauty, where every page brings a new story of wonder and excitement.

# Chapter One: Getting to Know Alaska

Welcome to your ultimate gateway to the Last Frontier! Within the pages of this travel guide for 2024-2025, you're embarking on an unforgettable journey into the heart of Alaska. From transportation tips to navigating the state's diverse outdoor attractions, discovering museum treasures, finding cozy accommodations, diving into Alaska's rich history, savoring its delectable cuisine, packing essentials, and uncovering the top attractions with addresses – this guide is your trusty companion for every step of your adventure.

Whether you're seeking serene wilderness or thrilling urban experiences, this book covers it all. You'll find detailed information about accommodations, including prices and addresses, making it a breeze to plan your stay. Alongside, valuable resources and recommendations are peppered throughout these pages, guiding you toward hidden gems and must-visit destinations.

Expect a treasure trove of insights, from the best hiking trails offering panoramic vistas to secret fishing spots hidden within vast landscapes. This guide is your key to discovering Alaska's heartbeat, from its charming small towns to the bustling cities.

You'll find detailed maps, insider tips, and all the essential information you need for a seamless and awe-inspiring journey.

With this guidebook in hand, you'll unlock the door to authentic Alaskan experiences. Discover the magic of Denali National Park, witness breaching whales in the Kenai Fjords, reel in a prized catch, and marvel at the rich cultural heritage of Alaska's native communities. This book is not just about places; it's about crafting unforgettable memories and connecting with Alaska's soul.

Furthermore, get ready to immerse yourself in Alaska's vibrant festival scene and cultural events. Detailed insights, including dates and times, await you, ensuring you do not miss the unique celebrations that define this remarkable state.

Alaska isn't just a place; it's an experience waiting to be lived. With this comprehensive guide, you'll uncover the soul of Alaska – its breathtaking landscapes, diverse cultures, and a tapestry of experiences. So, get ready to explore, embrace adventure, and create unforgettable memories as you embark on your journey through the wonders of the Last Frontier.

**Here's some handy information about Alaska:**

- *Country: United States of America*
- *Region: Alaska is a state in the northernmost part of the United States, situated in the northwest extremity of the North American continent.*
- *Capital: Juneau*
- *Largest City: Anchorage*
- *Area Code: +1 (same as the United States)*
- *Currency: United States Dollar (USD)*
- *Time Zone: Alaska Time Zone (AKT) - UTC-9:00 (AKST) during standard time and UTC-8:00 (AKDT) during daylight saving time.*
- *Official Language: English*
- *Main Industries: Oil and gas, tourism, fishing, timber, mining, and aerospace.*
- *Notable Natural Features: Glaciers, mountains, wildlife, national parks, and the Northern Lights (Aurora Borealis).*
- *Major Airports: Ted Stevens Anchorage International Airport (ANC) in Anchorage, Fairbanks International Airport (FAI) in Fairbanks,*

*and Juneau International Airport (JNU) in Juneau are among the largest airports in the state.*

## Climate of Alaska

Alaska is a land that dazzles with its incredible wildlife and rich natural resources.

But let's face it, it's a place of extremes. At the same time, the Indigenous communities have flourished there for thousands of years; folks from outside grapp with the harsh realities of its icy cold weather, long periods of darkness, rough storms, wild animal encounters, and tough limitations for farming or raising animals.

The weather in Alaska is super changeable, mostly due to ocean currents. The western coast gets warmed up by the Alaska Current, bringing in warmer water from the Pacific that moves up north and west along the southern Aleutian Islands.

Then, this warmer water cruises east along the northern coast of the Aleutians and dives into the Bering Sea. All this warm and cold water mixing together in the ocean also creates a low-pressure area in the sky known as the Aleutian low.

On the flip side, Alaska's Arctic coast feels the cold from an icy, westward-flowing ocean current.

Alaska isn't just one-size-fits-all when it comes to weather. It's got different climate zones (aside from its mighty mountains), and here's a quick look:

Southern Coastal and Southeastern Alaska, Gulf of Alaska Islands, and Aleutian Islands:

In summers, it's about 40 to 60 °F (4 to 16 °C), while winters hover around 20 to 40 °F (-7 to 4 °C).

Rain is all over the place, from 60 to 160 inches (1,500 to 4,000 mm). But some spots like Cordova-Valdez and bits of the west-central panhandle get mega rain—like Valdez, where 200 inches (5,100 mm) of snow is just another day. Oh, and the Aleutian Islands are famous for these sudden mega winds called williwaws.

## Alaska's Interior:

Gets a continental-style climate, especially cold air from Canada and Siberia in winter.

Summers swing between 45 to 75 °F (7 to 24 °C), while winters can go from 20 to -10 °F (-7 to -23 °C). But hey, sometimes summers hit the 90s F (about 34 °C) or winters plummet to the -60s F (about -54 °C).

Summers also bring a lot of thunderstorms that can start forest fires from all that wild lightning. Anchorage has gentler winters and cooler summers compared to the rest, with about 15 to 20 inches (380 to 500 mm) of rain each year.

## Islands and Coast of the Bering Sea:

Summers are kinda 40 to 60 °F (4 to 16 °C), and winters dip to about 10 to 20 °F (-12 to -7 °C).

Once you go past the Pribilof Islands, the Pacific's influence chills out, and the place gets iced up every winter.

Storms from the North Pacific often hit the coast, sometimes flooding it. And those gusty winds and blizzards from the storms? They're not easy on the fishing boats.

These weather zones bring their own flavor to Alaska, shaping its landscapes, critters, and even cool stuff like the Northern Lights. Up north, the Beaufort Sea helps keep things chill in the Arctic coastal lowland, also known as the North Slope.

## Summer and Winter Temperatures:

In the Arctic region, summers bring temperatures of roughly 35 to 55 °F (2 to 13 °C), while winters plunge to an average of -5 to -20 °F (-21 to -29 °C). Frequent storms whipped up by the polar easterlies result in high winds and snow blowing around, adding to the challenging conditions.

Precipitation and the environment in this area are unique.

There's around 5 to 10 inches (125 to 250 mm) of precipitation, which usually means a lot of snow but also some rain, especially in August.

This contributes to a waterlogged environment because there's not much evaporation, and the ground stays frozen (permafrost). In the summer, the Arctic enjoys 24-hour daylight. But because the sun's at a low angle, the ground only thaws around 1 foot (0.3 meters) deep. In contrast, during the sunless winter, the ice cover can reach a minimum of 1,000 feet (300 meters) thick and sticks around for about nine months along the northern coast.

## Climate Change Impact:

Since 1979, Alaska has been experiencing a warming trend in its climate, leading to the gradual melting of permafrost. This thawing has been noticeable and concerning.

The reduction in the thickness of the Arctic Ocean's pack ice and its retreat towards the north during summers are opening up possibilities for new navigation routes like the Northwest and Northeast passages via the Bering Strait in the summer months. However, this change isn't all positive.

It poses a serious threat to the habitats of polar bears, as well as their primary food source—seals. Additionally, the increased presence of bowhead whales in the Beaufort Sea during summer months faces potential disruption due to these changing conditions.

The warming temperatures have also influenced the migration patterns of several fish species, prompting them to move northward along Alaska's Pacific Coast.

These ongoing transformations in the Arctic region have significant implications for its ecology, the habitats of various wildlife, and potential changes in navigational routes. These changes underscore the far-reaching impacts of climate change on Alaska's environment, emphasizing the urgent need for measures to address and mitigate its effects.

## Plant and animal life

*Boreal forest in Alaska*

In southern regions like the panhandle and islands, lush forests are dominated by Sitka spruce, hemlock, Alaskan cedar, and other evergreen trees.

In contrast, the interior landscapes are primarily characterized by black spruce (Picea mariana) and white spruce (P. glauca), forming what's known as a climax forest community well-suited to the area's natural progression. Birch, willow, and aspen trees also thrive in these interior areas.

## musk oxen

When it comes to musk oxen, the islands in the Bering Sea, such as St. Lawrence, Nunivak, St. Matthew, and the Pribilof group, boast a unique Arctic maritime environment. Covered in tundra and surrounded by sea ice in winter, these islands are home to the largest herds of fur-bearing seals and sea otters worldwide. They also support populations of sea lions and walrus. Particularly noteworthy is Nunivak Island, which houses a protected population of musk oxen.

## Alaska: moose

Alaska's interior, notably Denali National Park and Preserve, is a haven for diverse wildlife. Brown and grizzly bears, caribou (also known as reindeer), wolves, and moose are among the notable inhabitants here.

During the summer months, substantial herds of caribou reside on the North Slope. These caribou undertake migratory journeys from the Brooks Range to the Arctic coastal plain for breeding.

The windy conditions in this region play a crucial role in insect control and offer better visibility for caribou, helping them spot wolves, their primary predators, from afar.

Both the interior and Arctic coastal plain also serve as nesting grounds for numerous migratory bird species, attracting large populations during their nesting seasons.

## People of Alaska

## Population composition

*Tlingit clan*

For thousands of years before Danish explorer Vitus Bering set foot in Alaska in 1741, a diverse array of Indigenous groups called the region home. Various Indigenous communities thrived across different areas.

The Tlingit and Haida peoples lived in the southern and southeastern coastal regions, while the Unangax (Aleut) occupied the Aleutian Islands and the western Alaska Peninsula.

Along the Bering shore and Arctic Ocean coast, the Inuit and Yupiit (Yupik) made their homes, and several Athabaskan-speaking communities resided in the interior.

The Tsimshian people of Metlakatla migrated to Alaska from British Columbia in the late 19th century. As per the 2020 census, American Indians and Alaska Natives make up around 16 percent of the state's population.

The population of Alaska reflects a rich diversity of ethnicities, including military personnel and their families.

The state's place names, influenced by early explorers, showcase a mix of English, Russian, Spanish, and French origins from various European countries.

The Russian-American Company was responsible for bringing the first Christian missionaries to Alaska. Among these, Innocent Veniaminov, later known as Metropolitan Innocent of Moscow and later canonized, was a prominent figure.

The Russian Orthodox Church played a pivotal role in converting many Alaska Natives to Christianity.

Presently, the main cathedral of the Russian Orthodox Church is located in Anchorage, with other significant Orthodox churches in Unalaska and Sitka. Kodiak hosts one of the few Russian Orthodox seminaries in the United States.

Alongside Orthodox Christianity, various Christian denominations like Roman Catholicism, Episcopalianism, and other smaller religious communities, including Jewish populations and followers of different faiths, coexist across the state. Moreover, traditional beliefs, known as shamanism, continue to exist alongside these other faiths without any significant conflicts.

## Settlement patterns

Settlement patterns reveal that over three-fifths of Alaska's population resides in the Greater Anchorage–Kenai Peninsula area.

This region is notable for its relatively milder temperatures, proximity to the sea, accessible ice-free ports, and significant developments in the petroleum and natural gas industries. It also serves as a central transportation hub for air, road, and rail networks.

Additionally, major Alaskan banks, corporations, and federal and state administrative agencies are headquartered in this area.

## Juneau, Alaska

More than one-eighth of Alaska's population calls the Greater Fairbanks area home, which includes the town of Delta Junction.

Historically known as a key hub for gold mining, Delta Junction holds significance as the endpoint of the Alaska Railroad, connecting Seward to Fairbanks.

Additionally, the larger cities in the south coastal archipelago and the Gulf of Alaska islands, including Ketchikan, Petersburg, Sitka, and Juneau, along with their surrounding regions, house a significant portion of Alaska's residents.

These areas are well-known as hubs for fishing and tourism activities across the state.

## Kodiak

Many Alaskans live in small communities positioned along rivers, highways, or the coastline, especially in the Arctic and western Alaska regions.

Key settlements like Barrow (situated at Point Barrow), Kotzebue, Nome, Bethel, Dillingham, Kodiak, and Unalaska have experienced significant population growth since the latter part of the 20th century. Barrow is particularly noteworthy as the main hub of the North Slope and holds the distinction of being the northernmost town in the United States. Notably, it has received substantial tax revenues from the oil operations in Prudhoe Bay.

# Demographic trends

The first significant migration wave from the contiguous United States, often referred to as the "Lower 48" by Alaskans, to Alaska occurred during the 1880s.

This period coincided with the discovery of gold and the establishment of fish canneries in the region. Later on, the construction of the Alaska Railroad and the growth of copper mining operations at Kennecott further attracted settlers during the 1920s and '30s.

During World War II, Alaska played a crucial military role as an important outpost. It served as a base for launching attacks against the Japanese, who had invaded parts of the Aleutian island chain. Additionally, Alaska provided military support to Russia, especially combat aircraft.

Following World War II, population growth was tied to the establishment of several military bases and the development of petroleum and natural gas resources in the Kenai Peninsula and Cook Inlet. After gaining statehood in 1959 and with the advancement of the Prudhoe Bay oil fields in the 1970s, Alaska experienced significant population expansion for about two decades. However, this growth trend somewhat stabilized in the 1990s.

In the early 21st century, nearly three-fifths of Alaska's residents were born outside of the state.

During this time, the percentage of foreign-born Alaskans increased to almost 8 percent, up from 6 percent in 2000. Most of these immigrants came from countries like Mexico, Canada, Korea, Japan, China, Germany, and Colombia.

Alaska boasts one of the youngest populations among U.S. states, with a median age of 35.5 years in 2019, compared to the national median age of 38.4 years. In the 2000 census, around 7 percent of Alaskans were aged over 65, roughly half of the U.S. average.

However, according to the 2020 census, this demographic group grew to 12.5 percent, approximately three-fourths of the U.S. average, signifying a significant increase in the elderly population within the state.

# Economy of Alaska

## Trans-Alaska Pipeline

The Alaskan economy is significantly influenced by its continuous status as a frontier. Challenges like high labor and transportation costs, as well as complex environmental and land-use regulations, have historically discouraged external investment.

However, significant improvements in infrastructure have notably reduced the expenses linked with economic activities.

Alaska faced a challenge with its limited tax base until the discovery of the North Slope oil fields in 1968.

This discovery led to the establishment of the Trans-Alaska Pipeline, which created job opportunities and significantly increased state revenue.

Presently, Alaska's economy predominantly relies on various key sectors, including oil production, fishing, federal and state expenditures (both civilian and military), research and development initiatives, and the tourism industry.

These sectors play crucial roles in driving economic growth within the state.

# Agriculture, forestry, and fishing

Alaska possesses over 3 million acres (1.2 million hectares) of land suitable for cultivation, but agriculture forms only a small part of the state's economy, leading to heavy reliance on food imports.

Despite attempts by the government in the 1970s to encourage agricultural growth, there hasn't been a significant expansion of cultivable land since then.

Commercial farming, involving crops like barley and potatoes and raising livestock such as cows and pigs, is concentrated in specific regions.

The Matanuska-Susitna Valley, north of Anchorage near Delta Junction southeast of Fairbanks, and, to a lesser extent, the Kenai Peninsula, are key areas for commercial farming.

Fairbanks also supports substantial small-scale farming, taking advantage of the long hours of summer sunlight for quick growth of vegetables, potatoes, and grains.

Livestock farming occurs on Kodiak Island, sheep farming on Unimak Island, and local caribou farming in the Kotzebue region.

Alaska also produces feed for a growing number of horses used for recreational purposes, hunting, and guided trips. Bison (buffalo) imported initially are sometimes harvested in the Delta Junction region.

Hunting, especially for moose and caribou, and fishing and whaling activities in the Beaufort and Chukchi seas are vital to the subsistence economy of Indigenous communities in Alaska.

The majority of Alaska's commercial timber resources are located in the Tongass and Chugach national forests, respectively, in the panhandle and along the southern coast. Strict logging regulations limiting timber leases led to the closure of pulp mills in Sitka and Ketchikan in the 1990s, causing a significant decline in timber-related activities and exports in Alaska. Efforts to establish an export-focused forestry industry in the Tanana Valley have not been successful.

## Alaska: commercial fishing

Alaska boasts one of the most robust commercial fishing industries in the United States, with Kodiak's port ranking among the largest nationwide.

A considerable portion of Alaska's fish production is exported, with various types of salmon holding significant importance. Salmon packing centers are situated in Ketchikan, Kodiak Island, Unalaska, Bristol Bay, and Prince William Sound. Additionally, commercial fishing fleets haul in substantial quantities of herring, cod, pollock, and halibut, as well as Dungeness, king, and Tanner crabs.

Fishing operations in Alaska's waters adhere to regulations set within the 200-mile-wide exclusive economic zone. Additionally, international fishing management in these areas involves agreements such as the U.S.-Canadian Pacific Salmon Treaty, initiated in 1985, and collaborative efforts between the U.S. and Russia regarding Bering Sea fisheries.

Aquatic farms in Alaska are engaged in harvesting oysters and clams, adding to the state's diverse seafood production.

# Resources and power

### Alaska: gold rush

Alaska boasts a rich history in hard-rock ore mining that dates back to 1880, with more than 90% of mined minerals comprising gold, copper, zinc, and silver.

Prospectors today continue their efforts using modern scientific techniques and aerial exploration methods. Some of the noteworthy mines in the state include the Fort Knox and Pogo gold mines near Fairbanks, as well as the Red Dog zinc mine close to Kotzebue.

Moreover, there is a significant molybdenum deposit near Ketchikan that remains untapped.

Another prominent mining site is the Greens Creek Mine, situated near Juneau, which is recognized as one of the largest sources of silver in the United States.

In addition to silver, this mine also yields lead, zinc, copper, and gold.

## Alaska History

Alaska's history traces back to around 10,000 BCE when people inhabited the land. During this ancient period, a land bridge connected Siberia to eastern Alaska, enabling the migration of people who followed herds of animals across this bridge.

Many of these early migrant groups, such as the Athabaskans, Unangan (Aleuts), Inuit, Yupiit (Yupik), Tlingit, and Haida peoples, have maintained their presence and cultural heritage in Alaska over thousands of years.

The exploration of Alaska began as early as 1700 when Indigenous peoples in Siberia mentioned the existence of a vast land lying due east. In 1728, an expedition commissioned by Tsar Peter I (known as Peter the Great) of Russia, led by Danish explorer Vitus Bering, confirmed the presence of this land.

However, due to fog, the expedition failed to locate North America. Bering's second voyage in 1741 led to the sighting of Mount St. Elias, and men from the expedition were sent ashore.

The discovery of sea otter furs during this expedition initiated a prosperous fur trade between Europe, Asia, and the North American Pacific coast over the following century.

## Russian settlement

The first European settlement in Alaska was established in 1784 by Russians at Three Saints Bay, near present-day Kodiak. Unfortunately, the arrival of Russian fur traders brought significant hardships to the Unangan people.

Many Unangan individuals suffered from violence at the hands of the newcomers or were exploited in the fur seal hunting industry. Additionally, diseases introduced by the Russians had devastating impacts on the Unangan population.

Initially serving as Alaska's capital, Kodiak was later replaced by Sitka in 1806 as the headquarters of the Russian-American Company, established in 1799 under the charter from Emperor Paul I.

The company, led by chief manager Aleksandr Baranov, was attracted to Sitka due to the abundant sea otter population in the area.

Baranov faced challenges, including conflicts with the Tlingit people at Old Harbor near Sitka. However, his successful establishment of Novo-Arkhangelsk (now Sitka) in 1804, after the battle of Sitka, marked a turning point despite conflicts between Alaska Natives and Europeans.

The Alaska Native Claims Settlement Act of 1971 partially addressed some of the land rights advocated by Alaska Natives.

While earlier Russian fur traders had strained relationships with Indigenous groups, the Russian-American Company maintained comparatively positive relations with the Unangan and Indigenous peoples in the southeast, as well as the Yupiit of the lower Yukon and Kuskokwim river valleys. Interactions included intermarriage between Unangan individuals and Russians, leading to conversions to the Russian Orthodox faith.

Some Unangan individuals, carrying Russian surnames, were employed by the Russian-American Company.

During this era, British and American merchants competed with the company, leading to disputes among fur traders. These disputes were resolved in 1824 when Russia signed separate treaties with the United States and Great Britain, establishing trade boundaries and commercial regulations. The Russian-American Company continued to govern Alaska until the region's purchase by the United States in 1867 through the Alaska Purchase.

## U.S. possession

The declining sea otter population and the impacts of the Crimean War (1853–1856) were key factors influencing Russia's decision to sell Alaska to the United States. The negotiations for the purchase were led by U.S. Secretary of State William H. Seward, who secured a treaty with the Russian minister to the United States.

Despite facing significant public opposition, Seward's proposal of $7.2 million for the territory was eventually approved by the U.S. Congress. On October 18, 1867, the American flag was raised in Sitka, officially marking the acquisition of Alaska. Initially called "Seward's Folly" by skeptics who doubted its value, the purchase reportedly led to the creation of the dessert "baked Alaska" to commemorate the occasion.

Upon becoming a U.S. possession, Alaska was governed by military commanders from the War Department until 1877, with limited internal development during this period. However, the establishment of a salmon cannery in 1878 marked the beginning of what became the world's largest salmon industry.

In 1884, Congress designated Alaska as a judicial land district, introducing federal district courts and establishing a school system. Alaska's first nonvoting delegate to Congress was elected in 1906, and in 1912, Congress established the Territory of Alaska, incorporating an elected legislature.

Concurrently, gold discoveries unfolded across various regions, including the Stikine River in 1861, Juneau in 1880, and Fortymile Creek in 1886. The rush to the Atlin and Klondike placer goldfields in neighboring British Columbia and Yukon territory between 1897 and 1900 led to the rise of new Alaska towns like Skagway and Dyea (now a ghost town), serving as entry points to the Canadian sites.

Subsequent gold discoveries in Nome in 1898 attracted prospectors from Canada and in Fairbanks in 1903.

These gold rushes highlighted Alaska's economic potential, prompting the development of major hard-rock gold mines in the panhandle. Additionally, copper was discovered in McCarthy in 1898, while gold dredging operations commenced in the Tanana River valley in 1903 and continued until 1967.

In 1903, the United States and Canada settled a border dispute concerning the boundary between British Columbia and the Alaska panhandle through the Alaska Boundary Tribunal. The tribunal supported the U.S. view that the border should follow the crest of the Boundary Ranges. By 1913, much of the border mapping had been completed based on this decision. Subsequently, significant railway developments occurred, including the construction of a narrow-gauge railroad connecting Skagway to Whitehorse in the Yukon via White Pass and the Cordova-to-McCarthy line along the Copper River.

The Alaska Railroad, an essential project, began operations in 1923, connecting Seward with Anchorage and Fairbanks, spanning around 500 miles (800 km).

In 1935, the government launched a farming initiative in the Matanuska Valley near Anchorage, establishing dairy cattle herds and crop farming. Similar agricultural efforts were extended to the Tanana and Homer regions.

During World War II in 1942, Japanese forces invaded Agattu, Attu, and Kiska islands in the Aleutian chain, conducting bombings at Dutch Harbor on Unalaska. This prompted the construction of large airfields and the Alaska Highway, a road stretching over 1,500 miles (2,400 km) linking Dawson Creek, British Columbia, to Fairbanks. Both projects significantly contributed to the state's commercial development.

Throughout the war, the U.S. Army relocated most of the Unangan from the Aleutian Islands, assigning them to work in canneries, sawmills, hospitals, schools, or internment camps in Juneau or the southeastern islands. Many Unangan people fell victim to diseases like influenza and tuberculosis during this period.

After the war, numerous Unangans returned to the Aleutians, while others chose to stay in southeastern Alaska.

## Alaska since statehood

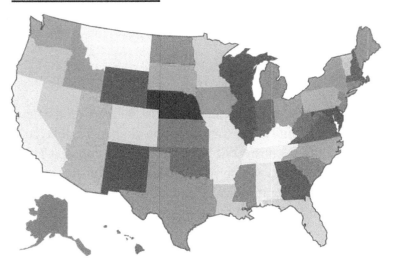

In 1946, Alaskans voted in favor of statehood, adopting a constitution in 1956. This decision culminated in Alaska becoming the 49th state of the United States in 1959 after Congressional approval of the statehood bill.

Alaska experienced numerous significant earthquakes in the 20th century, with the most devastating being the 1964 Alaska earthquake. This quake caused widespread destruction in parts of Anchorage, triggered a tsunami in Valdez, and led to significant coastal changes in Kodiak, Seward, and Cordova.

In the mid-20th century, oil and natural gas discoveries in the Kenai Peninsula and Cook Inlet initiated the state's leading mineral industry by the 1970s. The 1960s saw the emergence of a pulp industry in the panhandle, though mills in Ketchikan and Sitka ceased operations in the 1990s due to logging constraints.

The discovery of petroleum in Arctic lands in 1968 offered economic promise, but transportation challenges delayed its exploitation. Controversies surrounded the proposed Trans-Alaska Pipeline, which was eventually constructed and commenced operation in 1977, enabling the transport of oil from Prudhoe Bay to Valdez.

However, the infamous Exxon Valdez oil spill in 1989 resulted in extensive damage to Prince William Sound's marine ecology and local economy. This catastrophe was followed by other oil-related disasters, fueling debates between conservation and oil exploration.

In the early 21st century, declining oil production prompted discussions about drilling in sensitive areas like the Arctic National Wildlife Refuge and the Beaufort and Chukchi seas. U.S. government policies fluctuated between Democratic and Republican administrations, leading to bans, lifts, and suspensions on oil and gas development in these regions.

However, Alaska's journey through statehood and its economic development has been punctuated by seismic events, resource discoveries, and environmental concerns that continue to shape its trajectory.

## Culture and Traditions

Alaska's cultural diversity, blending the artistic traditions of its Indigenous communities and the influence of Russian heritage, profoundly shapes its modern culture.

Artistic expressions in Alaska are vibrant, particularly within Indigenous communities known for their exquisite ivory and wood carvings.

The art of totem carving, once nearly lost, has experienced a revival and is prominently showcased at Sitka National Historical Park.

Basketry and beadwork also hold significant importance among Alaska Natives, highlighting their artistic prowess and cultural heritage.

Alaska's landscape and allure have inspired a rich tapestry of literature.

Notable figures, such as Jack London, were drawn to Alaska during the Klondike gold rush in the nearby Yukon territory in the late 1890s. London's works, including "Call of the Wild" (1903), "White Fang" (1906), and "Burning Daylight" (1910), are set in Alaska and remain influential. Naturalist John Muir extensively explored Alaska's wilderness, documenting his adventures in "Travels in Alaska" (1915). Journalist John McPhee recounted his Alaskan journey in "Coming into the Country" (1977). "On the Edge of Nowhere" (1966) by James Huntington, narrating his life as the son of a white trapper father and Athabaskan mother, stands as another significant piece of Alaskan literature. Velma Wallis, an acclaimed Athabaskan writer, is known for several remarkable books, notably "Two Old Women" (1994). These literary works portray the diverse and captivating essence of Alaska's culture and history.

## Cultural institutions

Juneau is home to Alaska's historical library and state museum, housing extensive historical collections. The University of Alaska Fairbanks hosts the Museum of the North, a renowned research museum dedicated to Alaska's heritage.

Among its features is a permanent exhibit that explores the captivating natural phenomenon of the northern lights. Sitka boasts the Sheldon Museum and Cultural Center, which is committed to safeguarding and honoring the diverse heritage of Alaska Natives from the southeast region.

### Exit Glacier

Alaska is home to the nation's primary Arctic wilderness, facilitating extensive research in areas such as glacier, mountain, and tundra ecosystems, as well as atmospheric and ionospheric conditions and polar oceanography. This research is carried out by federal agencies, state institutions, universities, and private organizations.

The University of Alaska plays a crucial role in Arctic research, conducting comprehensive studies through institutions like the Geophysical Institute, Institute of Marine Science, Institute of Arctic Biology, and related groups. Since 1946, the Juneau branch of the Foundation for Glacier and Environmental Research, in collaboration with the National Science Foundation, the University of Idaho, and the University of Alaska, has supported research on the Juneau Icefield, focusing on glaciology and environmental sciences training.

In Seward, the Alaska SeaLife Center serves as the state's only public aquarium and operates as a center for rescuing ocean wildlife. Moreover, it is a significant research facility for studying marine life, attracting visitors due to its dual role as a research center and tourist destination.

## Sports and recreation

The official state sport in Alaska is dogsled racing, encompassing various events ranging from short sprints to extensive long-distance journeys.

The Iditarod Trail Sled Dog Race, established in 1967, has grown from a 25-mile (40 km) race to an impressive 1,100-mile (1,770 km) competition.

Every July in Fairbanks, the World Eskimo-Indian Olympics bring together Indigenous peoples from Alaska, Canada, and the Pacific Northwest to participate in traditional Alaskan games.

The University of Alaska Fairbanks and the University of Alaska Anchorage actively engage in diverse sports, including men's and women's basketball, skiing, and men's hockey.

The University of Alaska Anchorage initiated the Great Alaska Shootout basketball tournament in 1979 to bolster its men's basketball program, attracting notable National Collegiate Athletic Association (NCAA) teams until its conclusion in 2017.

Since the 1960s, the Alaska Baseball League has attracted top collegiate baseball players for summer exhibitions. With teams in Anchorage, Palmer, Chugiak, and Kenai, the league's highlight is the annual Midnight Sun Game, showcasing the athletes' talents in a unique setting.

## Tongass National Forest

Alaska provides numerous opportunities for outdoor activities across its diverse regions. The state encompasses several national wildlife refuges managed by the U.S. Fish and Wildlife Service, covering over 77 million acres (31 million hectares).

In 1980, an additional 100 million acres (40.5 million hectares) were designated for national parks, preserves, wildlife refuges, and wilderness areas, supplementing the already established 7.5 million acres (3 million hectares). Fairbanks hosts an annual ice-carving festival, one of the largest in the world, drawing visitors each year.

In the realm of media and publishing, major newspapers such as the Anchorage Daily News, Fairbanks Daily News-Miner, and Juneau Empire serve the state alongside various local and weekly newspapers.

Alaska also boasts a range of radio and television stations, with widespread access to cable and satellite television services.

## Chapter Two: Planning Your Trip

## When to Visit

Alaska, known for its breathtaking landscapes, unique wildlife, and fascinating cultural heritage, offers an array of experiences throughout the year, each season bringing its own allure and adventures.

Deciding when to visit Alaska depends largely on personal preferences, interests, and what you hope to experience. Each season offers its own set of advantages and considerations, making Alaska a year-round destination worth exploring.

## Spring:

*March-May*

Spring in Alaska, particularly from March through May, marks a transition period characterized by melting snow, emerging wildlife, and the start of milder temperatures. It's a time of renewal and offers unique experiences for travelers. However, it's essential to be prepared for unpredictable weather, including occasional snowfall and chilly temperatures.

Imagine embarking on a springtime journey in late March. You witness the magical sight of snow melting and daylight slowly returning after the winter darkness.

There's an air of excitement as wildlife begins to emerge. You might spot bears, moose, and migratory birds in the early stages of their return, making it an ideal time for wildlife enthusiasts and photographers.

## Activities:

Wildlife Viewing: The Kenai Peninsula, Denali National Park, and Southeast Alaska provide ample opportunities for observing wildlife awakening from winter hibernation.

Northern Lights: Although less common than in winter, there's still a chance to catch the Northern Lights before the midnight sun arrives.

Outdoor Adventures: Depending on snow conditions, you can still enjoy snowshoeing, cross-country skiing, and even dog sledding in some regions.

## Summer:

*June - August*

Longer days, abundant wildlife, blooming flowers, and a surge in outdoor activities characterize summer in Alaska, from June to August.

This season offers the warmest temperatures and the peak of tourist activity due to its accessibility and favorable weather conditions.

Consider visiting in July. The sun barely sets, creating the phenomenon of the midnight sun, allowing for extended daylight hours to explore and enjoy the natural beauty. The landscapes transform into vibrant greenery, and wildlife becomes more active, offering excellent opportunities for sightseeing and outdoor adventures.

## Activities:

**Wildlife Cruises:** Take advantage of boat tours to see whales, sea otters, and seabirds along the coastlines.

**Fishing:** Experience world-class fishing for salmon, halibut, and trout in rivers, lakes, and the ocean.

**Hiking and Camping:** Explore the vast wilderness, hike through national parks, or camp under the midnight sun.

**Fall:**

*September - November*

Fall in Alaska, spanning from September to November, brings stunning foliage, fewer crowds, and unique experiences. As temperatures begin to drop, this season showcases the breathtaking colors of autumn and provides opportunities to witness the natural spectacle of the Northern Lights.

*Imagine traveling in early September.*

The landscapes transform into a canvas of red, orange, and gold hues as the leaves change color. Wildlife becomes more active, preparing for winter, and it's an excellent time for observing the Northern Lights as the nights grow longer.

**Activities:**

**Foliage Tours**: Witness the breathtaking fall foliage, especially in regions like Denali, Talkeetna, and the Kenai Peninsula.

**Northern Lights Viewing:** As darkness returns, the Aurora Borealis becomes more visible, offering stunning displays.

**Off-Season Discounts:** Enjoy reduced rates and fewer crowds at accommodations and tours compared to the summer peak season.

## Winter:

*December - February*

Winter in Alaska, from December to February, is a wonderland blanketed in snow, offering unique experiences suited for adventurers seeking a different kind of beauty. It's the best time to witness the Northern Lights, partake in winter sports, and indulge in cultural festivities.

Picture traveling in January, enveloped in a winter wonderland.

The landscape is covered in snow, offering opportunities for thrilling winter sports like skiing, snowboarding, snowmobiling, and ice fishing. The Northern Lights illuminate the dark skies with dazzling displays, creating an otherworldly atmosphere.

## Activities:

**Northern Lights Chasing:** The long, dark nights provide optimal conditions for viewing the mesmerizing auroras.

**Winter Sports:** Enjoy a wide range of activities like dog sledding, ice climbing, skiing, and soaking in natural hot springs.

**Festivals and Events:** Immerse yourself in winter festivals, such as the Fur Rendezvous in Anchorage or the Iditarod Trail Sled Dog Race in March.

Alaska's diverse seasons offer unique experiences and adventures, making it a year-round destination. The best time to visit greatly depends on personal preferences, desired activities, and what you wish to explore. Whether you're seeking the midnight sun, the Northern Lights, wildlife encounters, or thrilling outdoor activities, each season in Alaska presents its own set of wonders and opportunities for discovery. No matter the time of year, Alaska welcomes visitors with its awe-inspiring landscapes and unique cultural heritage, promising an unforgettable journey into the heart of the Last Frontier.

## Packing Essentials

Packing for a trip to Alaska requires thoughtful consideration due to its diverse climate and range of activities available throughout the year. Here's a comprehensive breakdown of essential items categorized by various needs:

**Clothing:**

*Cold Weather Gear:*

- **Insulated Jacket**: Waterproof and insulated for warmth.
- **Fleece or Wool Layers:** To provide insulation under jackets.
- **Thermal Base Layers:** Moisture-wicking for warmth and comfort.
- **Waterproof Pants:** For protection against rain and snow.
- **Warm Hats, Gloves, and Scarves:** Essential for protecting extremities.
- **Winter Boots:** Waterproof, insulated, and suitable for cold conditions.

*Moderate Weather Gear:*

- **Light Jackets or Sweaters:** For cooler days or evenings.

- **Comfortable Pants and Jeans:** Suitable for various activities.
- **Comfortable Footwear:** Sturdy shoes or boots for walking and hiking.

### *Outdoor Gear:*

*Winter Activities:*

- **Snow Gear:** Skiing, snowboarding, or snowshoeing equipment.
- **Ice Cleats or Traction Devices:** For slippery surfaces.
- **Winter Sports Accessories:** Ski poles, goggles, helmets, etc.

### Summer Activities:

- **Hiking Boots or Trail Shoes:** Sturdy footwear for trekking.
- **Backpack or Daypack:** For carrying essentials during hikes.
- **Sun Protection Gear:** Sunscreen, sunglasses, and hats for UV protection.
- **Insect Repellent:** Essential for areas with mosquitoes.

**Travel Essentials:**

- **Travel Backpack or Suitcase**: Consider sturdy and waterproof options.
- **Reusable Water Bottle**: Hydration is crucial, especially during outdoor activities.
- **Travel Adapters/Converters:** For charging electronic devices.
- **First Aid Kit:** Include basic medical supplies.
- **Portable Power Bank:** For charging devices on the go.

*Miscellaneous*:

- **Camera or Smartphone:** Capture stunning landscapes and wildlife.
- **Binoculars:** Ideal for wildlife viewing.
- **Multi-tool or Swiss Army Knife:** Handy for various situations.
- **Reusable Bags:** Useful for shopping and carrying items.

*Documents:*

- **Valid Identification:** Driver's license or passport.
- **Travel Insurance Documents:** Important for emergency situations.
- **Printed Maps:** Useful for navigating remote areas.

### Personal Care:

- **Toiletries:** Toothpaste, toothbrush, shampoo, soap, etc.
- **Prescription Medications**: Sufficient supply and prescriptions.
- **Hand Sanitizer and Wet Wipes:** For cleanliness during outdoor activities.

### Weather-Specific Items:

- **Umbrella or Rain Poncho:** For protection against rain.
- **Sun Hat or Rain Hat:** Depending on the weather forecast.

Packing for Alaska should consider the diverse weather conditions and planned activities. Layered clothing suitable for cold temperatures, along with gear for outdoor adventures, is essential.

Tailor your packing list according to the season and specific activities you plan to engage in to ensure a comfortable and enjoyable trip to this beautiful and diverse destination.

# Chapter Three: Getting Around
## Transportation Options

## I. Overview of Transportation in Alaska

Alaska's transportation system is a unique network influenced by the state's vast size, challenging terrain, and diverse geographic features. Meeting transportation needs in Alaska is complex due to the expansive wilderness, extreme weather conditions, and remote communities.

The transportation infrastructure caters to various modes of travel due to the state's large geographical area, accommodating both urban centers and rural regions. Given Alaska's distinct characteristics, a combination of air, road, water, and rail transport is crucial for connecting communities and facilitating movement within the state.

Each mode of transportation plays a significant role in Alaska's accessibility and connectivity. The state's transportation system is a vital lifeline for residents, industries, tourism, and commerce. From navigating through mountainous terrains to traversing icy waters and remote areas, Alaska's transportation network is as diverse as its landscape.

## II. Air Transportation in Alaska

**Airports and Air Travel:** Alaska boasts a vast network of airports, including international, regional, and rural airstrips, facilitating domestic and international travel. Anchorage's

Ted Stevens Anchorage International Airport and Fairbanks International Airport serve as major hubs for domestic and international flights. Numerous regional airports connect remote communities, often accessible only by air.

**Airlines and Connectivity:** Several airlines operate within Alaska, providing passenger and cargo services. Alaska Airlines, Ravn Alaska, and smaller regional carriers offer flights connecting major cities, remote towns, and villages. Bush planes and small aircraft are integral for reaching off-the-grid areas.

**Bush Flying and Remote Access:** Bush flying plays a crucial role in reaching remote and isolated regions where road access is limited or absent. Small aircraft and bush pilots are indispensable for transporting goods, medical supplies, and passengers to inaccessible locations, especially in rural Alaska.

Air transportation in Alaska plays a pivotal role in linking distant communities, providing essential services, and supporting the state's economy. The unique challenges and vastness of Alaska's terrain make air travel a vital aspect of transportation for both residents and visitors.

## *III. Water Transportation in Alaska*

**Marine Travel and Ferries:** Alaska's extensive coastline and numerous waterways make maritime travel a significant mode of transportation. The Alaska Marine Highway System (AMHS) operates ferries, linking coastal communities, towns, and cities. These ferries provide essential connections and scenic voyages along the Inside Passage and other maritime routes. The iconic ferry journey from Bellingham, Washington, to Skagway, Alaska, via the Inside Passage is a popular route for travelers.

**Cruise Ships:** Alaska's tourism industry flourishes with cruise ships navigating the Inside Passage, offering travelers an incredible experience to witness stunning landscapes, glaciers, and wildlife along Alaska's coast. Ports of call like Juneau, Ketchikan, and Skagway are key stops on many cruise itineraries.

***Commercial Shipping and Cargo:*** Alaska's ports, such as Anchorage, Juneau, and Dutch Harbor, play a vital role in commercial shipping and cargo transportation. These ports handle goods, resources, and commodities vital to the state's economy, including seafood, minerals, and oil.

Boating and Personal Watercraft: Boating enthusiasts find ample opportunities for recreational boating, kayaking, and canoeing along Alaska's rivers, lakes, and coastal areas. Many residents utilize boats as a means of transport in remote regions with water access.

Water transportation in Alaska offers unique and scenic travel experiences and essential connections for remote communities and serves as a crucial conduit for trade, tourism, and recreational activities.

## *IV Road Transportation in Alaska*

## **Highway System Overview**

Alaska's road network provides essential connections between cities, towns, and wilderness areas, offering various opportunities for road travel.

## Alaska's Major Highways

**Alaska Highway (Alcan):** This iconic highway connects Alaska with Canada and the contiguous United States. It stretches over 1,300 miles, starting from Dawson Creek in British Columbia, Canada, and ending in Delta Junction, Alaska. The route traverses breathtaking landscapes, including the wilderness of Yukon and British Columbia.

**Parks Highway:** Stretching around 323 miles, this highway links Anchorage with Fairbanks. It offers access to Denali National Park and Preserve, showcasing stunning vistas and wildlife.

**Richardson Highway:** Running approximately 368 miles from Valdez to Fairbanks, the Richardson Highway provides access to historic towns, mountain passes, and natural wonders like the Worthington Glacier.

**Seward Highway:** Connecting Anchorage with the scenic town of Seward, this highway spans around 127 miles and offers spectacular views of the Turnagain Arm and Chugach Mountains.

## Challenges of Road Travel in Alaska

Traveling by road in Alaska presents certain challenges:

**Weather Conditions:** Harsh winter conditions, snowstorms, ice, and limited daylight hours in winter can affect road conditions.

**Remote Areas:** Many areas lack cell phone reception and services, especially in remote regions or on certain highways.

Wildlife Hazards: Wildlife, including moose and bears, might pose hazards, particularly during certain seasons.

# Car Rentals and Driving Tips

**Car Rentals:** Rental car services are available in major cities like Anchorage, Fairbanks, and Juneau. Reservations can be made online or through rental agencies.

**Driving Tips:**

**Weather Awareness**: Check weather forecasts before traveling and be prepared for changing weather conditions.

**Road Conditions:** Stay updated on road conditions and closures, especially in winter months.

**Wildlife Caution:** Watch for wildlife while driving, especially during dusk and dawn.

**Emergency Kit:** Keep an emergency kit with essentials like food, water, warm clothing, and a flashlight in your vehicle.

**Fuel Availability:** Plan refueling stops as gas stations can be scarce on remote routes.

# Rail Transportation in Alaska

Rail transportation in Alaska primarily revolves around the Alaska Railroad, which serves as a vital mode of travel, offering scenic and practical journeys for both locals and tourists.

# Alaska Railroad

The Alaska Railroad is the main rail service in the state, covering approximately 470 miles of track. It runs from Seward in the south to Fairbanks in the north, passing through Anchorage, Whittier, and Denali National Park along the way.

**Route:** The Alaska Railroad's main line runs through some of the most breathtaking landscapes in the state, including coastal areas, mountains, and wilderness.

**Trains:** The railroad operates several types of trains, including luxury dome cars, standard passenger cars, and scenic observation cars, offering different levels of comfort and views.

**Services:** The Alaska Railroad provides both scheduled passenger services and freight services, supporting local communities and tourism.

## Scenic Train Journeys

**Several scenic train journeys are offered by the Alaska Railroad:**

**Coastal Classic:** This route travels between Anchorage and Seward, showcasing stunning coastal views, glaciers, and wildlife.

**Denali Star:** The Denali Star travels between Anchorage and Fairbanks, passing through Denali National Park. Passengers can enjoy spectacular mountain vistas and potentially spot wildlife.

**Glacier Discovery:** Operating between Anchorage and Whittier, this route offers views of glaciers and fjords along the way.

## Passenger Services and Routes

**Passenger Services:** The Alaska Railroad provides different levels of service, including standard, GoldStar, and Adventure Class, offering various amenities and views.

**Routes:** The routes cover different regions of Alaska, highlighting diverse landscapes, wildlife, and natural wonders. Passengers have the option to choose routes based on their interests and time constraints.

**Booking and Timetables:** Reservations for the Alaska Railroad can be made online, through their website, or at various stations. Timetables vary seasonally, with more frequent services during the tourist season.

## Accessing Transportation Services and Ticketing

**Air Travel Ticketing:** Accessing flights in Alaska primarily occurs through ticket bookings from airlines operating in the state. Major airports like Ted Stevens Anchorage International Airport, Fairbanks International Airport, and Juneau International Airport are served by several domestic and international airlines. Ticket purchases can be made online through the airline's website or through travel agencies.

**Rail Ticketing:** The Alaska Railroad offers passenger services connecting Anchorage, Fairbanks, and Seward, among other destinations. Ticket reservations for train travel can be made online through the Alaska Railroad website, over the phone, or in person at their ticket offices or authorized agents.

**Ferry Reservations:** For the Alaska Marine Highway System (AMHS) ferries, reservations can be made online via the AMHS website, by phone, or in person at AMHS terminals. Passengers can book cabins or select seats for their journey, and tickets are generally priced based on the length of the trip, passenger type (adult, child, senior), and vehicle size (if applicable).

**Cruise Ship Bookings:** Reservations for cruises to Alaska can be made directly through cruise line websites, travel agencies specializing in cruise vacations, or by contacting the cruise line's customer service. The ticket prices vary based on the cruise duration, cabin type, itinerary, and additional amenities offered on board.

**Cargo and Commercial Shipping:** Ticketing for cargo shipping typically involves direct coordination with shipping companies or freight carriers. Commercial shipments are usually handled through contracts or agreements between businesses and shipping service providers.

**Boat Rentals and Water Tours:** Individuals seeking boat rentals or water tours often book tickets or make reservations through local tour operators, marinas, or recreational boating companies. These tickets can usually be purchased online or in person at the respective rental or tour agencies.

Ticketing for transportation services in Alaska generally involves making advance reservations, especially during peak seasons. Prices and availability vary, so it's advisable to book tickets well in advance, particularly for travel during popular tourist seasons like summer. Would you like further details on any specific aspect of ticketing or booking transportation in Alaska?

## Renting Vehicles and Driving Tips

*Car Rental Companies in Alaska*

### 1. Enterprise Rent-A-Car

Enterprise Rent-A-Car is one of the largest car rental companies in Alaska, offering a wide selection of vehicles to suit various travel needs. With multiple locations across the state, including Anchorage, Fairbanks, and Juneau, Enterprise provides convenient services for both airport and city pickups.

Travelers can choose from a range of vehicles, including economy cars, SUVs, minivans, and luxury cars. Enterprise offers competitive rates, often including unlimited mileage options, roadside assistance, and additional coverage packages for peace of mind during the rental period.

## 2. Hertz

Hertz is a well-known car rental company with branches in major cities and airports in Alaska. With a fleet of well-maintained vehicles, Hertz provides options ranging from compact cars to spacious SUVs and trucks suitable for various terrains.

Travelers can opt for Hertz Gold Plus Rewards for added benefits, including faster checkout services, exclusive discounts, and the ability to earn points for future rentals. The company offers flexible rental durations, including daily, weekly, and monthly options, along with affordable rates and optional insurance coverage.

## 3. Avis

Avis Car Rental operates in numerous locations throughout Alaska, catering to tourists, business travelers, and locals. Offering a diverse range of vehicles, including fuel-efficient cars, luxury vehicles, and SUVs, Avis allows customers to book online or through their mobile app for convenient reservations. Avis provides competitive rates, promotional discounts, and loyalty programs such as Avis Preferred, allowing members to skip the counter and access special offers. The company also offers additional services like GPS navigation systems and child safety seats for rental cars.

## 4. Budget Car Rental

Budget Car Rental is a popular choice for travelers seeking affordable and reliable vehicle options in Alaska. With multiple offices situated in major cities and airports across the state, Budget provides a range of vehicles suitable for solo travelers, families, or groups. Customers can select from economy cars, convertibles, SUVs, and vans at competitive prices. Budget offers flexible rental periods, including daily and weekly rates, along with optional insurance coverage and roadside assistance for added convenience and peace of mind.

## 5. Alamo Rent A Car

Alamo Rent A Car provides hassle-free car rental services in Alaska, serving various locations, especially airports, making it convenient for travelers arriving by air. Alamo offers a variety of vehicles, from compact cars to larger SUVs and minivans, accommodating different travel preferences. The company offers features like self-service kiosks, online check-in options, and express pickup services to expedite the rental process. Alamo's competitive rates, inclusive packages, and optional add-ons like GPS navigation systems or car seats make it a preferred choice for many travelers.

These major car rental companies in Alaska offer diverse vehicle options, convenient pickup locations, and additional services, making renting a car in Alaska a relatively straightforward process for visitors exploring the state's vast and scenic landscapes.

**Vehicle Options and Considerations for Car Rentals in Alaska**

**1. Types of Vehicles Available**

Alaska's car rental companies offer a diverse range of vehicles to suit different travel needs. Options typically include economy cars, compact cars, mid-size sedans, SUVs, trucks, vans, and luxury vehicles. The choice of vehicle depends on factors such as the number of passengers, luggage space needed, and the terrain to be traversed. SUVs and trucks are often preferred for travel on rougher terrains, while compact cars may be suitable for city driving and fuel efficiency.

**2. 4-wheel Drive and All-Wheel Drive Vehicles**

Given Alaska's diverse landscapes and varying weather conditions, many visitors opt for 4-wheel drive (4WD) or all-wheel drive (AWD) vehicles. These types of vehicles provide better traction and stability, making them suitable for navigating through snow, ice, and unpaved roads common in some regions of Alaska. Travelers planning to explore remote areas or venture off the main highways may find 4WD or AWD vehicles advantageous.

## 3. Vehicle Insurance and Additional Coverage

When renting a car in Alaska, it's essential to consider insurance and additional coverage options. Most car rental companies offer collision damage waivers (CDW) or loss damage waivers (LDW) that reduce or eliminate the renter's financial responsibility in case of damage or theft of the rental vehicle. Additionally, supplementary insurance coverage for personal accidents, roadside assistance, and theft protection may also be available for an extra fee. It's advisable to review the terms and conditions of insurance coverage carefully before making a decision.

## 4. Rental Costs and Fees

Rental costs and fees can vary based on factors such as the type of vehicle, rental duration, pickup location, and additional services requested. Daily or weekly rates are common, with the possibility of discounts for longer rental periods. Besides the base rental fee, travelers should inquire about additional charges like taxes, airport surcharges, underage driver fees, mileage limits, and fuel policies. It's recommended to compare prices among different rental companies and factor in all potential fees to determine the total cost of renting a vehicle in Alaska.

Considering these vehicle options and aspects can help travelers make informed decisions when selecting a rental car in Alaska, ensuring a suitable and cost-effective transportation choice for their journey through the state's stunning landscapes and diverse terrains.

## Reservation and Booking Process for Car Rentals in Alaska

### 1. Online Booking Platforms

Most car rental companies in Alaska offer convenient online booking platforms on their official websites or through third-party travel websites.

These platforms allow travelers to browse available vehicles, compare prices, and make reservations based on their preferences and travel dates. Online booking provides the flexibility of choosing pickup and drop-off locations, vehicle types, and additional services like insurance coverage or GPS navigation systems. Confirming reservations online often ensures the availability of preferred vehicles upon arrival.

### 2. Phone Reservations and Walk-Ins

For travelers who prefer personal assistance or have specific inquiries, many car rental companies in Alaska also offer phone reservation services. Calling the rental agency directly allows customers to speak with a representative, discuss rental options, clarify details, and make reservations over the phone. Additionally, some visitors may opt for walk-in bookings by visiting the rental office in person, especially if they haven't made prior arrangements or prefer to finalize details on-site.

## 3. Seasonal Availability and Rates

The availability of rental vehicles in Alaska can vary seasonally, with high demand during peak tourist seasons, such as summer months (May to September), when visitors flock to explore the state's natural beauty. During these times, booking in advance is advisable as it ensures a better selection of vehicles and often more competitive rates. Conversely, off-season travel, especially in winter, may offer lower rental rates due to decreased demand. However, travelers should note that weather conditions during winter might affect road accessibility and driving conditions.

Understanding the different booking options – whether online, via phone, or walk-ins – and considering seasonal availability and rates can assist travelers in securing their preferred rental vehicles efficiently and at competitive prices when exploring Alaska's captivating landscapes and attractions.

# Car Renting Company's Details

## Enterprise Rent-A-Car

- Address: 906 E 5th Ave, Anchorage, AK 99501, United States
- Phone: +1 907-277-1600
- Website: enterprise.com
- App: Available for download from the Google Play Store or Apple App Store. Search for "Enterprise Rent-A-Car."

## Hertz

- Address: 4940 W International Airport Rd, Anchorage, AK 99502, United States
- Phone: +1 907-243-4118
- Website: hertz.com
- App: Search for "Hertz Car Rental" in your app store (Google Play Store or Apple App Store) to download.

## Avis

- Location: Ted Stevens Anchorage International Airport
- Address: 5000 W International Airport Rd, Anchorage, AK 99502, United States
- Phone: +1 907-243-2377
- Website: avis.com
- App: Download the Avis app for Android or iOS devices from the respective app stores.

## Budget Car Rental

- Location: Ted Stevens Anchorage International Airport
- Address: 5000 W International Airport Rd, Anchorage, AK 99502, United States
- Phone: +1 907-243-0150
- Website: budget.com
- App: Find and download the Budget Car Rental app from the app stores.

## Alamo Rent-a-Car

- Location: Ted Stevens Anchorage International Airport
- Address: 5000 W International Airport Rd, Anchorage, AK 99502, United States
- Phone: +1 844-914-1558
- Website: alamo.com
- App: Install the Alamo mobile app from your app store (Google Play Store or Apple App Store).

Please note: Prices for rentals may fluctuate based on factors such as vehicle availability, rental duration, insurance options, seasonal demands, and ongoing promotions. For the most accurate and current information, review specific rental details and terms directly on their respective websites or apps.

# Chapter Four: Regions of Alaska
## I. Southeast Alaska

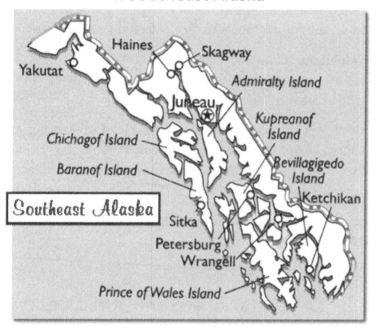

Southeast Alaska is known for its breathtaking landscapes, abundant wildlife, and thriving marine environments. Often referred to as the "Panhandle," this region is characterized by its intricate network of fjords, islands, and coastal rainforests. It's primarily accessible by air or water due to the absence of road connections to the rest of the state. This region boasts a temperate rainforest climate with heavy rainfall, contributing to its lush greenery and diverse ecosystems.

## Main Cities and Towns:

**Juneau:** The capital city of Alaska, nestled amidst the lush Tongass National Forest. It's not only the political center but also a hub for cultural activities and outdoor adventures.

**Ketchikan:** Known for its rich Native American totem pole culture, the city is often referred to as the "Gateway to the Inside Passage."

**Sitka** is a historical city offering a blend of Russian and Native Tlingit heritage. Sitka is home to the Sitka National Historical Park, preserving the area's cultural significance.

**Wrangell** is a charming town with a strong Native American heritage, offering various outdoor activities and historical sites.

# Notable Landmarks and Attractions

**Inside Passage:** A stunning waterway adorned with glaciers, islands, and abundant wildlife. It's a popular route for cruises, offering views of fjords, whales, and coastal wildlife.

**Tongass National Forest:** The largest national forest in the United States, offering pristine wilderness, hiking trails, and opportunities for wildlife viewing.

**Glacier Bay National Park:** A UNESCO World Heritage Site boasting spectacular tidewater glaciers, wildlife sightings, and stunning landscapes ideal for kayaking and photography.

**<u>Misty Fjords National Monument:</u>** A breathtaking wilderness area featuring deep fjords, towering cliffs, and serene lakes accessible by boat or floatplane.

Southeast Alaska's charm lies in its unique blend of natural beauty, indigenous culture, and outdoor recreational opportunities, making it a paradise for nature enthusiasts and adventurers alike.

# II. Southcentral Alaska
# Southcentral Alaska

Southcentral Alaska is a diverse and picturesque region that serves as a bustling hub for commerce, transportation, and outdoor adventure. It encompasses a variety of landscapes, from coastal areas along the Gulf of Alaska to the Chugach and Alaska mountain ranges. Anchorage, the state's largest city, is the focal point of the region, offering a unique blend of urban amenities amidst stunning natural surroundings.

## Main Cities and Towns:

**Anchorage:** The largest city in Alaska and a vibrant cultural and economic center. It features a range of attractions, museums, dining options, and access to outdoor activities.

**Wasilla:** Known for its proximity to recreational areas and as the hometown of the Iditarod Trail Sled Dog Race's official starting point.

**Palmer:** Renowned for its annual Alaska State Fair and agricultural roots, especially in farming and produce.

## Notable Landmarks and Attractions:

**Chugach State Park:** An extensive wilderness area surrounding Anchorage, offering hiking, camping, and stunning vistas of mountains, glaciers, and wildlife.

**Kenai Peninsula:** A stunning peninsula that juts into the Gulf of Alaska, known for its diverse wildlife, marine activities, and fishing opportunities.

**Matanuska Glacier:** A striking glacier easily accessible from Anchorage and Palmer, allowing visitors to explore ice caves and take guided hikes on the glacier.

**Prince William Sound:** A pristine area dotted with glaciers, fjords, and islands, ideal for kayaking, wildlife viewing, and marine tours.

Southcentral Alaska's unique blend of urban amenities, stunning landscapes, and outdoor recreational opportunities makes it an attractive destination for both residents and visitors seeking a perfect balance between city life and natural beauty.

## III. Interior Alaska

Interior Alaska is a vast and rugged region characterized by its subarctic climate, expansive wilderness, and rich cultural heritage. Spanning the area between the Alaska Range and the Brooks Range, this region is renowned for its extremes in weather, with bitterly cold winters and warm summers. It's a land of diverse ecosystems, including boreal forests, tundra, and numerous rivers and lakes.

**Main Cities and Towns:**

**Fairbanks:** The largest city in the Interior, known for its role in the Gold Rush, featuring a blend of modern amenities and a deep-rooted history. It's a gateway to the Arctic and offers stunning views of the Northern Lights.

**North Pole:** Famous for its festive Christmas-themed attractions and its proximity to Fairbanks, offering year-round holiday cheer.

**Delta Junction:** Situated at the intersection of the Alaska Highway and the Richardson Highway, marking the end of the Alaska Highway.

**Notable Landmarks and Attractions:**

**Denali National Park and Preserve:** Home to North America's highest peak, Denali (formerly Mount McKinley), offering breathtaking scenery, wildlife viewing, and hiking opportunities.

**Chena Hot Springs Resort:** A popular year-round destination boasting natural hot springs, outdoor activities like dog sledding and ice carving, and the chance to witness the Northern Lights.

**Alaska Pipeline:** A significant engineering marvel running across Interior Alaska, offering a glimpse into the state's oil industry and providing unique photo opportunities.

**<u>Tanana Valley State Fair:</u>** Held annually in Fairbanks, this fair showcases local agriculture, arts, crafts, and entertainment, drawing visitors from across the state.

The Interior is a fascinating blend of untamed wilderness and human ingenuity, offering visitors a chance to experience the grandeur of nature, witness Alaska's rich history, and immerse themselves in a variety of outdoor adventures throughout the year.

## IV. Southwest Alaska

Southwest Alaska is a region characterized by its unique blend of stunning landscapes, rich cultural heritage, and diverse wildlife. It spans a vast area encompassing the Bristol Bay coast, the Alaska Peninsula, and the Aleutian Islands. This region offers a mix of breathtaking scenery, vibrant Native cultures, and opportunities for outdoor exploration.

**Main Cities and Towns:**

**Bethel:** The largest community in the region, serving as a hub for the surrounding villages and known for its Indigenous culture and traditions.

**Dillingham** is a coastal city situated near Bristol Bay renowned for its commercial fishing industry and salmon runs.

**Kodiak:** The main city on Kodiak Island, famous for its bear viewing, fishing, and historical significance as the gateway to the Russian heritage in Alaska.

**Unalaska:** Located on the Aleutian Islands, it serves as a vital fishing port and is home to diverse wildlife, dramatic landscapes, and World War II history.

**Notable Landmarks and Attractions:**

**Katmai National Park and Preserve:** Known for its expansive wilderness, iconic brown bears, volcanic landscapes, and the Valley of Ten Thousand Smokes, a testament to the 1912 Novarupta eruption.

**Lake Clark National Park and Preserve:** Offers a mix of towering mountains, crystal-clear lakes, abundant wildlife, and cultural sites showcasing the Dena'ina Athabascan heritage.

**Aleutian Islands:** A chain of volcanic islands stretching across the Pacific Ocean, offering unparalleled opportunities for birdwatching, wildlife observation, and historical exploration.

**Togiak National Wildlife Refuge:** Famous for its diverse ecosystems, including tundra, forests, and rivers, providing habitats for wildlife like caribou, brown bears, and salmon.

Southwest Alaska is a treasure trove for adventurers, nature enthusiasts, and those seeking cultural immersion. Its awe-inspiring landscapes, rich history, and the warmth of its communities create an unforgettable experience for visitors.

# V. Arctic and Far North Alaska

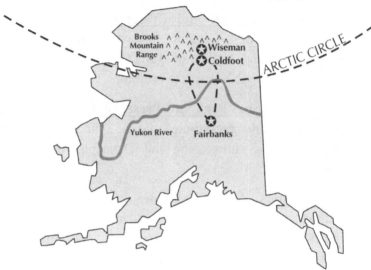

The Arctic and Far North region of Alaska is an expansive area characterized by its extreme climate, unique wildlife, and the cultural heritage of Indigenous communities. This remote and rugged territory extends above the Arctic Circle, offering a pristine wilderness teeming with Arctic flora and fauna.

**Main Cities and Towns:**

**Barrow (Utqiaġvik):** The northernmost city in the United States, serving as a cultural hub for Inupiat Eskimos and renowned for its traditional practices and subsistence lifestyle.

**Nome:** Known for its gold rush history, dog sledding traditions, and as the endpoint for the Iditarod Trail Sled Dog Race.

**Kotzebue:** A town on the shores of the Chukchi Sea, offering insights into Inupiat culture, dog mushing, and Arctic exploration.

**Utqiaġvik** (formerly known as Barrow): Notable for being the northernmost city in the United States, offering a unique perspective into Inupiat culture and traditions.

**Notable Landmarks and Attractions:**

**Gates of the Arctic National Park and Preserve:** An untouched wilderness characterized by rugged mountains, vast tundra, and pristine rivers, accessible only by air or foot.

**Arctic National Wildlife Refuge:** A pristine wilderness area known for its biological diversity, featuring tundra, coastal plains, and important habitats for diverse wildlife.

**Prudhoe Bay:** One of the largest oil fields in North America, offering a glimpse into Alaska's oil industry and Arctic ecosystems.

**Kobuk Valley National Park:** Famous for its sand dunes, caribou migrations, and the Kobuk River, providing ample opportunities for wilderness exploration.

The Arctic and Far North region of Alaska is a land of extreme beauty, embracing the harshness of the Arctic environment while preserving a unique cultural heritage and providing a glimpse into the natural world that few have the chance to experience.

## Chapter Five: Outdoor Attractions
## Top Attractions in Alaska

### I. Denali National Park and Preserve

D enali National Park and Preserve, situated in the interior of Alaska, is renowned for its awe-inspiring natural beauty, wildlife, and the majestic Denali (formerly Mount McKinley), North America's highest peak. Covering over 6 million acres of land, the park offers an unspoiled wilderness and a diverse ecosystem, making it a must-visit destination for nature enthusiasts, hikers, and wildlife lovers.

## Wildlife and Natural Beauty

The park is home to diverse wildlife, including grizzly bears, moose, wolves, Dall sheep, caribou, and numerous bird species. Visitors have the opportunity to witness these animals in their natural habitats. The landscape is dominated by Denali, reaching an elevation of 20,310 feet (6,190 meters) above sea level, surrounded by vast tundra, alpine forests, and glaciers, providing breathtaking views and ample photography opportunities.

## Activities and Visitor Centers

*Visitor Centers:*

A. **Denali Visitor Center:** Located near the park entrance, it offers exhibits, information, and orientation films about the park's natural history and ecosystems.

B. **Eielson Visitor Center:** Positioned at Mile 66 on Denali Park Road, providing stunning panoramic views of Denali and exhibits on the park's geology, wildlife, and weather.

## Activities:

a. **Scenic bus tours:** Various bus tours offer visitors a chance to explore the park's interior, offering wildlife sightings, spectacular landscapes, and the chance to witness Denali.

b. **Hiking trails:** With various skill levels available, hiking trails in the park provide opportunities for visitors to explore the wilderness, encounter wildlife, and immerse themselves in nature.

c. **Ranger-led programs:** Educational programs, guided walks, and talks by park rangers are available at different locations throughout the park.

**Address:**

Denali National Park and Preserve,

P.O. Box 9, Denali Park, AK 99755, United States

**Ticket & Open Time:**

The park is typically open year-round, but the main visitor services are available from mid-May to mid-September.

Entrance fees vary depending on the season and transportation chosen. The entrance fee for a private vehicle is around $15-$30 per person.

- Contact:
- Phone: +1 907-683-9532
- Website: https://www.nps.gov/dena/index.htm

Denali National Park and Preserve provides an unparalleled experience of Alaska's untamed wilderness, offering visitors a chance to immerse themselves in the beauty and grandeur of nature while exploring its diverse ecosystems and wildlife.

## II. Glacier Bay National Park and Preserve

Glacier Bay National Park and Preserve, located in southeast Alaska, is a UNESCO World Heritage Site renowned for its breathtaking natural beauty, magnificent glaciers, and diverse marine and terrestrial ecosystems. Encompassing over 3.3 million acres, the park offers visitors a unique opportunity to witness the powerful forces of glacial movement, explore the icy fjords, and observe an array of wildlife in their natural habitats.

## Glaciers and Fjords

**Glaciers:** The park is home to numerous tidewater glaciers, including the massive Margerie Glacier, Grand Pacific Glacier, and others. These glaciers are constantly calving, creating mesmerizing displays of ice breaking off into the bay, resulting in thunderous splashes.

**Fjords:** The park boasts stunning fjords carved by glaciers over thousands of years, offering breathtaking views of towering cliffs, serene waters, and impressive ice formations.

## Cruises and Visitor Information

**Cruises:** One of the most popular ways to experience Glacier Bay is by taking a cruise. Several cruise lines offer excursions that provide visitors with a chance to witness the glaciers up close, navigate through the bay's pristine waters, and spot diverse marine life, including whales, seals, and seabirds.

**Visitor Information:**

**Visitor Center:** The Bartlett Cove Visitor Center offers exhibits, information, and ranger-led programs, providing insights into the park's natural history, geology, and wildlife.

**Ranger-Led Programs:** The park offers various educational programs, guided walks, and talks led by rangers at different locations throughout the park.

Address:

Glacier Bay National Park and Preserve,

PO Box 140,

Gustavus, AK 99826, United States

**Ticket & Open Time:**

The park is open year-round, but visitor services are primarily available from late May to early September.

Entrance fees vary based on the mode of transportation. For a private vehicle, it's around $5 per person.

- Contact:
- Phone: +1 907-697-2230
- Website: https://www.nps.gov/glba/index.htm

Glacier Bay National Park and Preserve offers an extraordinary opportunity to witness the raw beauty of Alaska's glaciers, fjords, and diverse ecosystems, making it an essential destination for nature enthusiasts and those seeking unforgettable natural experiences.

## III. Kenai Fjords National Park

Kenai Fjords National Park, situated on the Kenai Peninsula in south-central Alaska, is renowned for its dramatic landscapes, abundant wildlife, and stunning fjords. Covering over 669,984 acres, the park showcases a diverse terrain of ice, ocean, and mountains, offering visitors a glimpse into the wonders of a glacially carved wilderness.

## Coastal Wilderness and Glaciated Valleys

**Glaciers:** The park features an array of awe-inspiring tidewater glaciers, including the renowned Exit Glacier. Witnessing these magnificent ice formations up close is a breathtaking experience.

**Fjords and Coastline:** The park's rugged coastline is dotted with deep fjords carved by ancient glaciers. Visitors can explore these scenic waterways, witness calving glaciers, and encounter marine life, such as whales, sea lions, and seabirds.

## Boat Tours and Hiking Trails

**Boat Tours:** Several tour operators offer boat excursions departing from Seward, allowing visitors to navigate through the park's icy waters, observe glaciers, and witness the richness of marine wildlife.

**Hiking Trails:** The park offers various trails catering to different skill levels, such as the Harding Icefield Trail, which offers stunning panoramic views of the icefield and surrounding landscapes. The Exit Glacier area also provides shorter trails for a closer look at the glacier.

Address:

Kenai Fjords National Park,

PO Box 1727,

Seward, AK 99664, United States

**Ticket & Open Time:**

Entrance fees vary based on the mode of transportation and age. The fee for a private vehicle is around $15 per person.

The park is accessible year-round, but visitor services and facilities may vary by season.

- Contact:
- Phone: +1 907-422-0500
- Website: https://www.nps.gov/kefj/index.htm

Kenai Fjords National Park offers a stunning combination of glaciers, fjords, and rich marine ecosystems, providing visitors with an unforgettable experience amid the captivating natural beauty of Alaska's wilderness.

## IV. The Inside Passage

The Inside Passage, a coastal route along the Pacific Ocean, is an iconic maritime path renowned for its breathtaking beauty, rich cultural heritage, and abundant wildlife. Stretching from Puget Sound in Washington State, through British Columbia, and up to the southeastern coast of Alaska, this intricate network of fjords, channels, and islands offers a scenic and captivating journey.

### Scenic Waterways and Islands

**Fjords and Channels:** The Inside Passage is characterized by its stunning fjords carved by ancient glaciers and intricate waterways, offering mesmerizing vistas of lush forests, snow-capped mountains, and sparkling waters.

**Islands:** Numerous islands speckle the passage, including the Alexander Archipelago in Alaska and islands like Vancouver Island in British Columbia, each presenting unique landscapes and cultural attractions.

## Wildlife Viewing and Cruises

**Marine Life:** The Inside Passage is a haven for diverse marine life, including whales, dolphins, sea lions, and sea otters. Observing these majestic creatures in their natural habitat is a highlight of the journey.

**Cruises and Tours:** Various cruise lines and tour operators offer voyages through the Inside Passage, providing travelers with the opportunity to explore its scenic beauty, witness wildlife, and experience the local culture of coastal towns and villages.

**Address:** The Inside Passage spans along the coastlines of Washington State, British Columbia, and Southeastern Alaska.

**Ticket & Open Time:** The Inside Passage does not have specific entry fees or operating hours as it comprises a vast network of waterways accessible via various ports and towns along the coast.

**Contact:** The primary points of contact for information and bookings are the cruise lines, tour operators, and visitor centers in the respective regions along the passage.

The Inside Passage stands as a testament to nature's grandeur, offering a remarkable journey through stunning landscapes, diverse wildlife, and cultural richness along the scenic coastal waterways of the Pacific Northwest.

## V. Mendenhall Glacier

The Mendenhall Glacier, a spectacular river of ice, is located in the Tongass National Forest near Juneau, Alaska. Spanning around 13 miles in length, it is part of the Juneau Icefield and stands as a breathtaking example of the region's glacial wonders.

### Glacial Ice and Recreation

**Glacial Majesty:** The glacier's colossal ice mass presents a stunning display of blue ice, crevasses, and towering ice walls. It offers a captivating insight into the dynamics of glacial formations.

**Outdoor Activities:** Visitors can engage in various recreational activities around the glacier, including hiking, kayaking, and wildlife viewing in the surrounding area. Adventurous explorers can also opt for guided glacier hikes and ice-climbing tours to experience the glacier up close.

## Visitor Center and Tours

**Visitor Center:** The Mendenhall Glacier Visitor Center offers educational exhibits, films, and interactive displays that provide insights into the glacier's formation, the local ecosystem, and the impact of climate change on glaciers.

**Tours and Access:** Guided tours, often led by knowledgeable park rangers, offer visitors an opportunity to explore the glacier's terminus and its stunning features. Access to the glacier might require transportation by boat or hiking trails.

**Address:** Mendenhall Glacier Visitor Center, 6000 Glacier Spur Rd, Juneau, AK 99801, United States.

**Ticket & Open Time:** Entry to the Mendenhall Glacier Visitor Center may have nominal fees, and specific open times can vary with the season. Please check the Tongass National Forest website or contact the visitor center for details.

**Contact:** For tour bookings, visitor information, and updates on glacier access, reach out to the Mendenhall Glacier Visitor Center at +1 907-789-0097 or visit the Tongass National Forest website for more details.

The Mendenhall Glacier serves as an awe-inspiring testament to the majesty of nature's icy wonders, offering visitors a chance to witness the grandeur of a glacier while providing educational insights into the significance of these natural formations.

## VI. Alaska Native Heritage Center

The Alaska Native Heritage Center, situated in Anchorage, Alaska, stands as a cultural hub showcasing the rich heritage, traditions, and lifestyles of Alaska's Indigenous peoples. It offers visitors a profound insight into the diverse cultures of Alaska's Native communities.

## Cultural Exhibits and Performances

**Cultural Heritage:** The center houses diverse exhibits and displays portraying the lifestyles, art, traditions, and history of Alaska's Indigenous groups, including Athabascan, Inupiaq, Yup'ik, Tlingit, Haida, and more.

**Performances:** Visitors can witness captivating performances that showcase traditional dances, music, storytelling, and other cultural expressions of Alaska Native communities. These performances often offer glimpses into age-old traditions and rituals.

## Workshops and Demonstrations

**Interactive Workshops:** The center conducts hands-on workshops and demonstrations, allowing visitors to engage in activities such as indigenous craft-making, storytelling, traditional games, and learning about subsistence practices.

**Guided Tours:** Guided tours led by knowledgeable guides provide in-depth insights into the various exhibits, providing a deeper understanding of Alaska's diverse Native cultures.

**Address:** Alaska Native Heritage Center, 8800 Heritage Center Dr, Anchorage, AK 99504, United States.

**Ticket & Open Time:** Admission fees might vary, and opening hours are subject to change. It's advisable to check the Alaska Native Heritage Center's official website or contact them directly for current ticket prices and operational hours.

**Contact:** For information on ticketing, guided tours, workshops, and performances, you can reach the Alaska Native Heritage Center at +1 907-330-8000 or visit their official website for more details and reservations.

The Alaska Native Heritage Center offers an enriching experience, allowing visitors to appreciate and honor the vibrant cultures, traditions, and history of Alaska's Indigenous peoples while partaking in educational and interactive activities.

## VII. Anchorage Museum

The Anchorage Museum stands as one of Alaska's premier cultural institutions, offering a multifaceted experience that explores art, history, science, and culture. Situated in downtown Anchorage, it serves as a hub for exhibitions, education, and community engagement.

## Art, History, and Science Exhibits

**Art Galleries:** The museum boasts diverse art collections, ranging from contemporary artworks to traditional Native Alaskan art, showcasing pieces by local, national, and international artists.

**History Exhibits:** Visitors can explore engaging exhibits that delve into Alaska's history, including its Indigenous cultures, explorations, and the state's development over time.

**Science Displays:** The museum features interactive science exhibits that highlight Alaska's unique natural environment, including geology, wildlife, and environmental science.

## Programs and Special Events

**Educational Programs:** The Anchorage Museum offers educational programs and workshops catering to all ages, fostering learning and creativity through hands-on activities, lectures, and seminars.

**Special Events:** Throughout the year, the museum hosts special events, including cultural festivals, film screenings, lectures by guest speakers, and community-centered activities.

**Address:** Anchorage Museum, 625 C St, Anchorage, AK 99501, United States.

**Ticket & Open Time:** Admission fees, operational hours, and special event schedules may vary.

Visitors are encouraged to check the Anchorage Museum's official website or contact them directly for updated ticket prices, hours of operation, and information on upcoming events.

**Contact:** For inquiries about tickets, programs, and special events, you can contact the Anchorage Museum at +1 907-929-9200 or visit their official website for detailed information and reservations.

The Anchorage Museum offers an immersive experience, combining art, history, and science to provide visitors with a comprehensive understanding of Alaska's rich cultural heritage, artistic expressions, and scientific exploration.

## VIII. Alaska Railroad

The Alaska Railroad is a renowned rail service that traverses through some of Alaska's most stunning landscapes, offering both residents and tourists an exceptional way to experience the state's natural beauty and diverse terrains via rail travel. Established in 1914, this railroad is a historic and integral part of Alaska's transportation system.

### Scenic Train Journeys

**Coastal Classic Route:** This route runs between Anchorage and Seward, showcasing breathtaking coastal views, glaciers, fjords, and mountain scenery along the way.

**Denali Star Route:** Traveling between Anchorage and Fairbanks, this journey is renowned for its views of Denali (formerly known as Mt. McKinley), river valleys, and diverse landscapes, including boreal forests.

**Glacier Discovery Route:** Connecting Anchorage to Whittier or Spencer Glacier, this route features awe-inspiring views of glaciers, wildlife, and the Chugach National Forest.

### Passenger Services and Routes

**Passenger Services:** The Alaska Railroad offers various passenger services, including Adventure Class, GoldStar Service, and Wilderness Express, each providing different levels of comfort, amenities, and scenic views.

**Routes and Schedules:** The railroad operates scheduled services along its various routes, offering both day trips and multi-day adventures for passengers to experience Alaska's diverse landscapes and attractions.

**Address:** Alaska Railroad Corporation, 327 W. Ship Creek Ave., Anchorage, Alaska 99501, United States.

**Ticketing and Reservations:** For information on ticket prices, schedules, and reservations for specific routes, travelers are encouraged to visit the Alaska Railroad's official website or contact them directly for updated details.

**Contact:** For inquiries, reservations, or any assistance, you can contact the Alaska Railroad at +1 800-544-0552 or visit their official website to book tickets and access travel information.

The Alaska Railroad presents an exceptional opportunity for travelers to immerse themselves in Alaska's natural wonders, offering scenic train journeys that traverse through some of the state's most picturesque landscapes and iconic attractions.

## IX. Iditarod Trail Sled Dog Race

The Iditarod Trail Sled Dog Race is an iconic and historic long-distance sled dog race that takes place annually in Alaska. Covering over a thousand miles, the race commemorates the historic "serum run" of 1925 when sled dog teams transported diphtheria antitoxin to Nome, saving the town's residents from a deadly outbreak.

### Historic Race and Dog Sledding Culture

**History:** The race typically begins in Anchorage or Willow and ends in Nome, Alaska. It honors the history and culture of dog sledding, showcasing the vital role sled dogs played in Alaska's past.

**Sled Dog Teams:** The race features professional mushers and teams of sled dogs navigating challenging terrains, extreme weather conditions, and remote Alaskan wilderness. It embodies the spirit of adventure, teamwork, and endurance.

### Race Routes and Visitor Information

**Routes:** The race covers a rugged and varied landscape, including frozen rivers, tundra, and mountain passes, offering a unique perspective of Alaska's wilderness.

**Visitor Information**: Spectators can witness the race's start in Anchorage or Willow, as well as checkpoints along the route. Nome is the final destination where the winning musher and dog team reach the finish line.

**Address:** The race spans across various Alaskan locations, starting from Anchorage or Willow and concluding in Nome, Alaska.

**Visitor Information:** To get detailed information about race schedules, routes, and spectator spots, visitors can refer to the official Iditarod Trail Sled Dog Race website or contact the Iditarod Trail Committee.

**Contact:** For inquiries or additional details, contact the Iditarod Trail Committee at +1 907-376-5155 or visit their official website for race updates and visitor information.

The Iditarod Trail Sled Dog Race is not only a competitive event but also a celebration of Alaska's sled dog culture, history, and the incredible bond between mushers and their dogs, attracting visitors from around the world to witness this extraordinary race across the Alaskan wilderness.

## X. Fairbanks and the Aurora Borealis

Fairbanks, Alaska, is renowned as one of the best places on Earth to witness the mesmerizing phenomenon of the Aurora Borealis, or Northern Lights. Situated in the heart of Alaska, Fairbanks offers incredible opportunities for viewing this natural wonder.

## Northern Lights Viewing and Science

**Aurora Borealis:** Fairbanks provides an ideal vantage point to witness the dazzling display of the Northern Lights. Visitors can experience vibrant curtains of green, purple, and red lights dancing across the night sky.

**Viewing Locations:** Popular sites for viewing the Aurora include Creamer's Field Migratory Waterfowl Refuge, Chena Lakes Recreation Area, or guided tours to remote locations.

**Science Behind the Lights:** Fairbanks also boasts scientific facilities and observatories, such as the Geophysical Institute at the University of Alaska Fairbanks, offering educational insights into the science behind the Aurora Borealis.

### Cultural Attractions and Winter Activities

**Cultural Experiences:** Fairbanks offers cultural attractions like the Museum of the North, showcasing Alaskan history, art, and native culture.

**Winter Activities:** Visitors can enjoy winter sports like dog sledding, ice fishing, and snowmobiling.

The Ice Museum, where intricate ice sculptures are displayed, is another highlight.

**Address:** Fairbanks, Alaska, offers various locations for Northern Lights viewing, with accommodations, tours, and attractions spread throughout the city.

**Visitor Information:** For detailed Northern Lights forecasts, viewing tips, and information on accommodations and tours, visitors can refer to the Explore Fairbanks website or contact the Fairbanks Visitors Center.

**Contact:** Explore Fairbanks can be reached at +1 907-456-5774 for inquiries or visit their official website for detailed information on Aurora viewing and winter activities.

Fairbanks is a hub for witnessing the breathtaking Aurora Borealis, combining natural wonders with cultural experiences and a host of winter activities, making it an unforgettable destination for travelers seeking the magic of the Northern Lights and Alaskan winter adventures.

## Cultural Events and Festival in Alaska

Alaska is rich in cultural diversity, and its vibrant tapestry of events and celebrations reflects the traditions, history, and heritage of its indigenous people as well as its modern multicultural society. Here is an extensive guide to cultural events in Alaska:

**1. Alaska Native Heritage Month**

**Description:** Alaska Native Heritage Month is a month-long celebration in November that honors and celebrates the diverse cultures, traditions, languages, and contributions of Alaska Native people. Various events, performances, workshops, and exhibitions take place across the state to showcase indigenous arts, crafts, music, dances, storytelling, and traditional practices.

**Location:** Various locations across Alaska, including Anchorage, Fairbanks, Juneau, and rural communities.

**Activities:** Cultural exhibitions, traditional music and dance performances, storytelling, arts and crafts demonstrations, and workshops on indigenous languages and traditions.

**Contact:** Alaska Native Heritage Center - Phone: +1 907-330-8000

Ticket: Admission fees may apply for certain events, while some activities are free.

**Time of Visit:** Throughout November.

### 2. Anchorage Folk Festival

*Description:* The Anchorage Folk Festival is an annual event that celebrates folk music, dance, and storytelling. Held in January, this festival gathers musicians, dancers, and storytellers from diverse cultural backgrounds to perform traditional and contemporary folk music, including bluegrass, Celtic, Americana, and world music. Workshops and jam sessions also provide opportunities for community engagement.

**Location:** Anchorage, Alaska

**Activities:** Live music performances, dance workshops, storytelling, jam sessions, dance parties, music workshops.

**Contact:** Anchorage Folk Festival - Email: info@anchoragefolkfestival.org

**Ticket:** Admission is often free or at a minimal cost for certain workshops.

**Time of Visit:** Typically held in late January.

### 3. Sitka Summer Music Festival

**Description:** The Sitka Summer Music Festival is an annual classical music festival that brings together world-class musicians to perform chamber music in the picturesque setting of Sitka. The festival includes concerts, recitals, masterclasses, and educational programs aimed at fostering appreciation for classical music.

**Location:** Sitka, Alaska

**Activities:** Chamber music concerts, recitals, masterclasses, educational programs, and workshops.

**Contact:** Sitka Summer Music Festival - Phone: +1 907-747-6774

**Ticket:** Tickets are available for individual concerts or festival passes.

**Time of Visit:** June through July.

## 4. Ketchikan Wearable Arts Show

**Description:** The Ketchikan Wearable Arts Show is an annual event that showcases wearable art creations by local artists and designers. This unique show features avant-garde fashion, costumes, textiles, and accessories made from unconventional materials, highlighting the creativity and craftsmanship of Alaskan artists.

**Location:** Ketchikan, Alaska

**Activities:** Runway fashion show, wearable art exhibitions, designer showcases, and auctions.

**Contact:** Ketchikan Area Arts and Humanities Council - Phone: +1 907-225-2211

**Ticket:** Tickets are available for the fashion show and exhibitions.

**Time of Visit:** Usually held in February.

## 5. Alaska Folk Festival

**Description:** The Alaska Folk Festival, held annually in Juneau, celebrates folk music and dance. This week-long event brings together musicians, dancers, and enthusiasts from around Alaska and beyond to participate in performances, workshops, and jam sessions focused on traditional and contemporary folk music genres.

**Location:** Juneau, Alaska

**Activities:** Live music performances, dance sessions, workshops, jam sessions, contra dancing.

**Contact:** Alaska Folk Festival - Email: info@akfolkfest.org

**Ticket:** Admission is often free for most events.

**Time of Visit:** Typically held in April.

**6. World Eskimo-Indian Olympics (WEIO)**

**Description:** The World Eskimo-Indian Olympics is a multi-day event that celebrates indigenous cultures and

traditional athletic games practiced by Alaska Native and indigenous people from around the circumpolar region. The event includes competitions such as the Eskimo stick pull, high kick, seal hop, blanket toss, and other athletic contests that test strength, agility, and endurance.

**Location:** Fairbanks, Alaska

**Activities:** Traditional games and competitions, cultural performances, crafts, and food vendors.

**Contact:** World Eskimo-Indian Olympics - Phone: +1 907-452-6646

**Ticket:** Tickets are available for daily or event passes.

**Time of Visit:** Usually held in July.

## 7. Fur Rendezvous (Fur Rondy)

**Description:** Fur Rendezvous, or Fur Rondy, is an annual winter festival in Anchorage that celebrates Alaskan culture, history, and traditions. The festival features a variety of events, including the iconic Running of the Reindeer, snow sculpture contests, sled dog races, a Native arts market, a carnival, and fireworks.

**Location:** Anchorage, Alaska

**Activities:** Reindeer races, sled dog races, snow sculpture contests, carnival rides, Native arts market, cultural performances, fireworks.

**Contact:** Anchorage Fur Rendezvous - Phone: +1 907-274-1177

**Ticket:** Tickets are required for some events; others may be free to attend.

**Time of Visit:** Usually held in late February.


## 8. Alaska State Fair

Description: The Alaska State Fair is a major annual event that celebrates agriculture, entertainment, arts, and culture. Held in Palmer, the fair features livestock exhibits, agricultural displays, competitive exhibits, live concerts, carnival rides, food vendors, arts and crafts, and various entertainment shows.

**Location:** Palmer, Alaska

**Activities:** Livestock exhibits, agricultural displays, live concerts, carnival rides, arts and crafts, food vendors, and entertainment.

**Contact:** Alaska State Fair - Phone: +1 907-745-4827

**Ticket:** Admission fees vary for different days and events.

**Time of Visit:** Usually held in late August through early September.

## 9. Celebration - Southeast Alaska Native Cultural Festival

**Description:** Celebration is a biennial cultural festival in Juneau that celebrates the indigenous cultures of Southeast Alaska. The event gathers Alaska Native tribes and communities to showcase traditional dance, music, art, crafts, regalia, and cultural practices. The celebration aims to preserve and promote the rich heritage of Alaska Native cultures.

**Location:** Juneau, Alaska

**Activities:** Dance performances, cultural exhibitions, art and craft demonstrations, storytelling, Native foods.

**Contact:** Sealaska Heritage Institute - Phone: +1 907-463-4844

**Ticket:** Tickets are available for various events and workshops.

**Time of Visit:** Usually held in odd-numbered years (e.g., 2023, 2025).

## 10. Nome Iditarod Fest

**Description:** The Nome Iditarod Fest is an annual festival that celebrates the finish of the legendary Iditarod Trail Sled Dog Race. This festivity includes cultural events, Native arts and crafts, live music, dog sled rides, and opportunities to meet mushers and their sled dog teams as they complete their epic journey.

**Location:** Nome, Alaska

**Activities:** Cultural events, arts and crafts, live music, dog sled rides, meet-and-greets with mushers.

**Contact:** Nome Visitor Center - Phone: +1 907-443-6623

**Ticket:** Free admission to most events.

**Time of Visit:** Usually held in March.

## 11. Alaska Bald Eagle Festival

**Description:** The Alaska Bald Eagle Festival takes place in Haines, celebrating the annual gathering of bald eagles along the Chilkat River. The festival offers eagle-watching tours, photography workshops, lectures, nature walks, and cultural presentations highlighting the significance of bald eagles in Alaskan culture and ecology.

**Location:** Haines, Alaska

**Activities:** Eagle-watching tours, photography workshops, nature walks, lectures, cultural presentations.

**Contact:** American Bald Eagle Foundation - Phone: +1 907-766-3094

**Ticket:** Tickets are available for guided tours and workshops.

**Time of Visit:** Usually held in November.

## 12. Whalefest

**Description:** Whalefest is an annual marine science festival in Sitka that celebrates the migration of whales and highlights marine conservation. The event includes lectures, workshops, art exhibits, film screenings, guided tours, and opportunities for whale watching and marine wildlife observation.

**Location:** Sitka, Alaska

**Activities:** Lectures, workshops, art exhibits, film screenings, guided tours, whale watching.

**Contact:** Sitka WhaleFest - Phone: +1 907-747-8878

**Ticket:** Admission fees may apply for certain events.

**Time of Visit:** Usually held in November.

These cultural events and festivals in Alaska offer a fantastic opportunity for visitors to experience the diverse cultures, traditions, and heritage of the state while enjoying entertainment, engaging in activities, and interacting with local communities. Events' dates and details are subject to change, so it's advisable to verify with the organizers or event websites for the most current information before planning a visit.

## 13. Anchorage International Film Festival (AIFF)

**Description:** The Anchorage International Film Festival is a showcase of independent films, documentaries, and short films from around the world. The festival includes screenings, filmmaker Q&A sessions, workshops, and networking opportunities promoting the art of cinema in Alaska.

**Location:** Anchorage, Alaska

**Activities:** Film screenings, filmmaker Q&A sessions, workshops.

**Contact:** Anchorage International Film Festival - Phone: +1 907-338-3700

**Ticket:** Tickets are available for film screenings and events.

**Time of Visit:** Usually held in early December.

## 14. Girdwood Forest Fair

**Description:** The Girdwood Forest Fair is a quirky and colorful celebration held in Girdwood. This fair features arts and crafts vendors, live music, local food stalls, a parade, and various family-friendly activities, creating a vibrant and festive atmosphere in the community.

**Location:** Girdwood, Alaska

**Activities:** Arts and crafts vendors, live music, local food stalls, parade, family-friendly activities.

**Contact:** Girdwood Forest Fair - Phone: +1 907-783-2323

**Ticket:** Free admission.

**Time of Visit:** Usually held on the first weekend in July.

These festivals offer visitors and locals alike a chance to immerse themselves in various cultural experiences, arts, entertainment, and community celebrations. Each event contributes to the rich tapestry of Alaska's diverse cultural landscape. Always check the specific dates and details of these festivals, as they might be subject to change from year to year.

## 15. World Ice Art Championships

**Description:** The World Ice Art Championships in Fairbanks is a globally renowned ice sculpting competition that showcases the skills of talented ice artists from around the world. Held in a winter wonderland setting, this festival features incredible ice sculptures of various themes and sizes, including single-block carvings and large-scale multi-block creations.

**Location:** Fairbanks, Alaska

**Activities**: Ice sculpting competitions, ice carving demonstrations, illuminated ice art displays, kids' activities, and photo opportunities.

**Contact:** Ice Alaska - Phone: +1 907-451-8250

**Ticket**: Tickets are required for entry; prices may vary depending on the day and activities.

**Time of Visit:** Typically held in February to March.

The World Ice Art Championships are a spectacular celebration of ice artistry, drawing visitors to witness the breathtaking beauty of these ephemeral ice sculptures created by talented artists, making it a must-visit event in Fairbanks during the winter months.

# Chapter Six: Accommodations in Alaska

## Types of Accommodations in Alaska

Alaska offers a diverse range of accommodations to suit various preferences, from luxurious hotels and resorts to rustic cabins and campgrounds. Each type of lodging provides a unique experience catering to different traveler needs and interests:

## A. Hotels and Resorts

**Description:** Alaska has a range of hotels and resorts catering to various preferences. From luxury establishments in cities to rustic lodges in remote areas, there's something for everyone.

**Price Range:** Prices vary depending on the location, amenities, and services offered. On average, expect prices ranging from $100 to $500 per night.

**Address:** Various locations across Alaska, including major cities like Anchorage, Juneau, and Fairbanks.

**Services:** Typically, hotels offer amenities such as Wi-Fi, parking, dining, concierge services, fitness centers, and more. Resorts often provide additional facilities like spas, outdoor activities, and guided tours.

## Luxurious Hotels in Alaska

Discover a selection of upscale accommodations nestled within the beautiful Alaskan landscape:

1. *The Lodge at Denali Park Village Hotel* – Embrace Wilderness Living

**Location:** Mile 231 Parks Hwy, Denali National Park and Preserve, AK 99755, USA

Situated along the banks of the scenic River Nenana, The Lodge offers a captivating retreat amidst 20 acres of verdant surroundings. Boasting elegantly furnished rooms with stunning river views, the hotel provides impeccable hospitality to its guests. Adventure enthusiasts can partake in a variety of exhilarating activities, including hiking, trekking, river rafting, camping, fishing, homestead tours, and helicopter rides, ensuring an exciting and fulfilling stay.

**Noteworthy Feature**: Guests can indulge in a Denali backcountry safari via 4-WD Jeep, available through advance booking.

**Starting Price:** $260/night

**Website** | https://www.denaliparkvillage.com/lodging/the-lodge/

2. *Top of the World Hotel* – Embrace the Vast Tundra Landscape

**Location:** 3060 Eben Hopson St, Utqiagvik, AK 99723, USA

For an authentic experience steeped in Eskimo culture, consider a stay at the Top of the World Hotel in Barrow. Among the finest hotels in Barrow, Alaska, this establishment offers a perfect blend of luxury and comfort. With breathtaking ocean views, spacious accommodations, delicious homecooked meals, and exceptional hospitality, this hotel provides a warm and inviting retreat.

**Noteworthy Feature:** The hotel offers a guest kitchen setup, allowing visitors to prepare their own meals.

**Starting Price:** $240/night

**Website** | http://www.tundratoursinc.com/

3. *Prospector Hotel* – A Pet-Friendly Haven

**Location: 375** Whittier St, Juneau, AK 99801, USA

Nestled within walking distance from Juneau's downtown area, the Prospector Hotel stands as one of the finest accommodations in Alaska, offering a splendid stay experience. Featuring spacious rooms, meeting facilities, covered parking, and complimentary WiFi, this hotel caters to every guest's needs. Whether you're traveling with your family or on a business trip, Prospector Hotel ensures a comfortable and convenient stay in Juneau.

**Noteworthy Feature:** Complimentary heritage coffee is offered to all guests.

**Starting Price:** $165/night

**Website** | https://prospectorhotel.com/

4. *The Hotel Alyeska* – Elegant and Convenient

**Location:** 1000 Arlberg Ave, Girdwood, AK 99587, USA

Set against a picturesque backdrop of mountains, hanging glaciers, and verdant forests, The Hotel Alyeska remains a preferred choice for those seeking a blend of luxury and natural beauty. Recognized with accolades such as the Certificate of Excellence and Hall of Fame by Trip Advisor, this award-winning hotel boasts a spa, yoga room, fitness studio, whirlpool, and a saltwater heated pool. Guests can relish local cuisine at the mountaintop Seven Glaciers restaurant and savor the in-room service of signature Starbucks coffee. Offering an exceptional stay, The Hotel Alyeska stands as one of the top-notch 5-star hotels in Alaska.

**Noteworthy Feature:** The Alyeska Aerial Tram, starting from the hotel, takes visitors up to the summit of Mount Alyeska, providing breathtaking views of snowy landscapes, glaciers, and lush mountains.

**Starting Price:** $155/night

**Website** | https://www.alyeskaresort.com/hotel

5. *Hotel Captain Cook* – A Classic Destination

**Location:** 939 W 5th Ave, Anchorage, AK 99501, USA

Nestled in the heart of Anchorage's downtown area, Hotel Captain Cook stands as a timeless accommodation option. Offering 546 beautifully appointed rooms and suites, along with the iconic Crow's Nest restaurant, this family-friendly hotel provides enchanting views of the harbor. Renowned for its exceptional service and warm hospitality, Hotel Captain Cook remains a top choice for families and couples seeking a memorable stay in Alaska.

**Noteworthy Feature:** The hotel houses a fully equipped Athletic Club, boasting a range of facilities such as a workout room, steam room, tanning beds, cycling studio, jacuzzi, and aerobics room.

**Starting Price:** $150/night

**Website** | http://captaincook.com/

6. ***Bridgewater Hotel*** – Affordable Comfort with Scenic River Views

**Location:** 723 1st Ave, Fairbanks, AK 99701, USA

Nestled in the heart of Fairbanks, Bridgewater Hotel offers a comfortable stay with breathtaking views of the Chena River. Known for its reasonable rates, warm hospitality, and delectable local cuisine, this hotel is surrounded by vibrant restaurants and shops, making it an ideal base to explore Fairbanks.

**Special Amenities:** Complimentary shuttle service from the airport and train station to the hotel.

**Starting Price:** $110/night

**Website** | http://www.bridgewaterhotel.ca/

7. ***Best Western Plus Edgewater Hotel*** – Affordable Luxury with Bay Views

**Location:** 202 5th Ave, Seward, AK 99664, USA

Offering picturesque views of the bay from its rooms, Best Western Plus Edgewater Hotel stands as an excellent choice for those seeking a longer stay in Seward, Alaska. Centrally situated, the hotel provides outstanding facilities and services to ensure every guest enjoys a comfortable and relaxing experience. While complimentary breakfast is offered, each room is equipped with a microwave and refrigerator for added convenience.

**Special Offerings:** Organized whale watching tours, kayaking, and fishing upon prior request.

**Starting Price:** $110/night

**Website** | https://www.bestwestern.com

8. ***Embassy Suites by Hilton Anchorage*** – Exceptional Personalized Attention

**Location:** 600 E Benson Blvd, Anchorage, AK 99503, USA

Embassy Suites by Hilton Anchorage offers modern amenities and top-notch services to its guests. This all-suite hotel features well-designed suites, some with majestic mountain views and private whirlpools. Their renowned in-house restaurant, Territory Kitchen and Bar, specializes in delicious Alaskan seafood delicacies. For those seeking a decent hotel in Alaska without breaking the bank, this is an excellent choice.

**Special Features**: Complimentary breakfast is provided, and the hotel also offers made-to-order breakfast for guests with specific preferences or dietary needs.

**Starting Price:** $100/night (approximate conversion from INR 7575)

**Website** | http://embassysuites3.hilton.com

## Budget Alaska Hotels

Here are comfortable yet affordable hotels in Alaska:

1. ***Driftwood Hotel*** – Comfort Redefined

**Location:** 435 W Willoughby Ave, Juneau, AK 99801-1786

Driftwood Hotel epitomizes Alaskan hospitality and is among the most sought-after budget-friendly hotels in Alaska. This 3-story hotel boasts 62 spacious rooms, including one and two-bedroom suites equipped with kitchens stocked with a microwave, refrigerator, coffee maker, and utensils. Offering facilities like free local calls, complimentary WiFi, printer, and fax services, Driftwood Hotel ensures all traveler needs are met.

**Special Highlights:** Organized fishing trips and on-site freezer facilities for storing the day's catch.

**Starting Price:** $83/night

**Website** | https://www.dhalaska.com/

2. *Anchorage Grand Hotel* – Boutique All-Suite Property

**Location:** 505 W 2nd Ave, Anchorage, AK 99501, USA

Anchorage Grand Hotel provides an affordable stay in downtown Anchorage, close to major city attractions like the Museum of History and Art, Performing Arts Center, and Convention Center. Originally built in 1950 and fully renovated in 2000, this hotel offers elevator access, vending machines for snacks and beverages, and complimentary on-site parking, setting it apart from other affordable accommodation options in Alaska.

**Special Features:** Complimentary packed breakfasts, including oatmeal, granola bars, juice, yogurt, bagels, and cream cheese, are delivered to the doorstep each morning.

**Starting Price:** $82/night

**Website** | https://www.anchoragegrand.com/

# B. Lodges and Cabins

**Description:** Alaska's lodges and cabins are known for their serene locations amidst nature. These accommodations offer a rustic yet comfortable stay, often in remote wilderness areas or near scenic spots.

**Price Range:** Rates can vary widely based on location and facilities, ranging from $80 to $300 per night.

**Address:** Spread throughout Alaska, particularly in regions like Denali, Kenai Peninsula, and remote areas.

**Services:** Lodges and cabins usually provide cozy interiors, kitchenettes, and outdoor facilities like barbecue areas, fire pits, and access to hiking trails or fishing spots.

Here are some lodges and cabins in Alaska, along with their city, addresses, and contact information:

## 1. Tutka Bay Lodge

**City:** Homer

**Address:** Tutka Bay Lodge, 44630 Sterling Hwy, Homer, AK 99603, USA

**Contact:** Phone: +1 907-274-2710

**Website:** https://withinthewild.com/lodges/tutka-bay-lodge/

## 2. Winterlake Lodge

**City:** Anchorage

Address: Winterlake Lodge, Anchorage, AK 99501, USA

Contact: Phone: +1 907-274-2710

Website: https://withinthewild.com/lodges/winterlake-lodge/

### 3. Talkeetna Alaskan Lodge

City: Talkeetna

Address: 23601 S Talkeetna Spur, Talkeetna, AK 99676, USA

Contact: Phone: +1 907-777-2805

Website: https://www.talkeetnalodge.com/

### 4. Kenai Fjords Glacier Lodge

City: Seward

**Address:** P.O. Box 1729, 1304 4th Avenue, Seward, AK 99664, USA

**Contact:** Phone: +1 907-777-2805

**Website:** https://www.kenaifjordslodge.com/

### 5. *Denali Backcountry Lodge*

**City:** Denali National Park

**Address:** P.O. Box 71380, Talkeetna, AK 99676, USA

**Contact:** Phone: +1 907-777-2805

**Website:** https://www.denalibackcountrylodge.com/

### 6. *McKinley Creekside Cabins*

**City:** Denali National Park

**Address:** Mile 224 George Parks Hwy, Denali National Park, AK 99755, USA

**Contact:** Phone: +1 907-683-2277

**Website:** https://mckinleycabins.com/

These lodges and cabins offer various amenities and activities while providing a chance to experience the beauty of Alaska's landscapes. Please check their websites or contact them directly for reservations, availability, and specific details about their services.

# C. Bed and Breakfasts (B&Bs):

**Description**: B&Bs offer a homely atmosphere and personalized service. They are often smaller, family-run establishments, providing a cozy and intimate experience.

**Price Range:** Prices typically range from $80 to $250 per night, varying with location and services provided.

**Address:** Scattered across Alaska, prominently in towns like Anchorage, Juneau, and Sitka.

**Services**: These accommodations offer comfortable rooms, homemade breakfast, and sometimes additional amenities such as guided tours or local insider tips from hosts.

Here are some Bed and Breakfasts (B&Bs) in Alaska, along with their locations, addresses, and contact information:

### 1. Camai Bed and Breakfast

**City:** Anchorage

**Address:** 3838 Westminster Way, Anchorage, AK 99508, USA

**Contact:** Phone: +1 907-337-2257

**Website:** https://www.camaibnb.com/

### 2. Alaska House of Jade Bed and Breakfast

**City:** Anchorage

**Address:** 3800 Delwood Pl, Anchorage, AK 99504, USA

**Contact:** Phone: +1 907-337-3477

**Website:** https://www.alaskahouseofjade.com/

### 3. *A Rabbit Creek Bed & Breakfast*

**City:** Anchorage

**Address:** 15930 Commons Ct, Anchorage, AK 99516, USA

**Contact:** Phone: +1 907-345-4590

**Website:** https://www.arabbitcreekbnb.com/

### 4. *Alaska Wolf House Bed and Breakfast*

**City:** Anchorage

**Address:** 1648 Eide St, Anchorage, AK 99501, USA

**Contact:** Phone: +1 907-272-4129

**Website:** https://www.alaskawolfhouse.com/

### 5. *Alaska European Bed & Breakfast*

**City:** Anchorage

**Address:** 3107 Cottonwood St, Anchorage, AK 99508, USA

**Contact:** Phone: +1 907-258-3803

**Website:** http://www.alaskaeuropean.com/

### 6. *Northern Nights Bed & Breakfast*

**City:** Anchorage

*Address:* 3361 Cottonwood St, Anchorage, AK 99508, USA

*Contact:* Phone: +1 907-258-6709

*Website:* https://northernnightsalaska.com/

These Bed and Breakfasts offer comfortable accommodations and a more intimate lodging experience, often with personalized service and local insights. You can visit their websites or contact them directly for reservations, availability, and specific details about their services.

## D. Vacation Rentals:

**Description:** Vacation rentals include apartments, cabins, or houses available for short-term stays. They are ideal for families or groups seeking a home-like experience.

**Price Range:** Prices can vary significantly based on size, location, and amenities, ranging from $100 to $500+ per night.

**Address:** Available in different parts of Alaska, particularly in tourist areas and cities.

**Services:** These rentals come equipped with kitchens and living spaces and may offer additional amenities like Wi-Fi, laundry facilities, and outdoor areas.

### 1. *Alyeska Hideaway Log Cabins*

**City:** Girdwood

*Address:* 1130 Timberline Dr, Girdwood, AK 99587, USA

*Contact:* Phone: +1 907-783-1000

*Website:* https://www.alyeskahideaway.com/

### 2. *Northern Lights Resort & Spa*

**City:** Fairbanks

**Address:** 1671 Steese Hwy, Fairbanks, AK 99712, USA

**Contact:** Phone: +1 907-389-2812

**Website:** https://www.alaskanorthernlights.com/

### 3. *Alaska's Lake Lucille Bed & Breakfast*

**City:** Wasilla

**Address:** 235 W Lake View Ave, Wasilla, AK 99654, USA

**Contact:** Phone: +1 907-357-0352

**Website:** https://www.alaskaslakelucille.com/

### 4. Diamond M Ranch Resort & RV Park

**City:** Kenai

**Address:** 48500 Diamond M Ranch Rd, Kenai, AK 99611, USA

**Contact:** Phone: +1 907-283-9424

**Website:** https://www.diamondmranch.com/

## 5. The Gakona Lodge & Trading Post

**City:** Gakona

**Address:** Mile 2 Tok Cutoff, Gakona, AK 99586, USA

**Contact:** Phone: +1 907-822-3482

**Website:** https://www.gakonalodge.com/

## 6. Trail River Gardens Bed & Breakfast

**City:** Moose Pass

**Address:** 41218 Seward Hwy, Moose Pass, AK 99631, USA

**Contact:** Phone: +1 907-288-3646

**Website:** https://trailrivergardens.com/

These vacation rentals offer diverse lodging options, from cabins and lodges to resorts and bed & breakfast accommodations. Each one provides unique experiences and amenities, allowing visitors to immerse themselves in Alaska's natural beauty and charm. For reservations or more information, you can visit their websites or contact them directly.

# E. Campgrounds and R.V. Parks

**Description:** Alaska boasts numerous campgrounds and R.V. parks, perfect for nature enthusiasts and travelers seeking a more outdoorsy experience.

**Price Range:** Rates range from $15 to $50 per night for campsites and $40 to $150+ per night for R.V. parks.

**Address:** Spread throughout Alaska's wilderness areas, national parks, and towns.

**Services:** Campgrounds offer basic facilities like tent spaces, fire pits, and communal restrooms. R.V. parks provide hookups, dump stations, and sometimes amenities like Wi-Fi and laundry.

These accommodation options cater to various preferences and budgets, allowing visitors to experience Alaska according to their desired style of stay.

Here are some campgrounds and R.V. parks in Alaska, along with their respective locations, addresses, and contact information:

### 1. *Denali Rainbow Village & RV Park*

**City:** Denali National Park

**Address:** Mile 238.6 Parks Hwy, Denali National Park and Preserve, AK 99755, USA

**Contact:** Phone: +1 907-683-7777

**Website:** https://denalirvpark.com/

## 2. *Klondike RV Park & Cabins*

**City:** Dawson City

**Address:** 1445 Front St, Dawson City, YT Y0B 1G0, Canada

**Contact:** Phone: +1 867-993-6777

**Website:** https://klondikerv.com/

### 3. Heritage RV Park

**City:** Homer

**Address:** 1945 E End Rd, Homer, AK 99603, USA

**Contact:** Phone: +1 907-235-7245

**Website:** https://www.heritagervpark.com/

### 4. River's Edge RV Park & Campground

**City:** Fairbanks

**Address:** 4200 Boat St, Fairbanks, AK 99709, USA

**Contact:** Phone: +1 907-474-0286

**Website:** https://www.riversedge.net/

### 5. *Seward Waterfront Park Campground*

**City:** Seward

**Address:** 1200 4th Ave, Seward, AK 99664, USA

**Contact**: Phone: +1 907-224-4011

**Website:** https://www.cityofseward.us/

### 6. *Chicken Gold Camp & Outpost*

**City:** Chicken

**Address:** 1/4 Mile Airport Rd, Chicken, AK 99732, USA

**Contact:** Phone: +1 907-235-6396

**Website:** https://www.chickengold.com/


These campgrounds and R.V. parks offer a range of amenities and settings, from riverside locations to proximity to national parks, providing opportunities for outdoor enthusiasts to experience the natural beauty of Alaska. For bookings or more details, you can visit their websites or contact them directly.

# Factors to Consider When Choosing Accommodations

When deciding on accommodations in Alaska, several crucial factors can significantly impact your stay and overall experience:

## A. Location:

*Proximity to Attractions:* Consider accommodations close to the specific attractions or activities you plan to explore. For instance, opting for lodges near national parks or waterfront cabins for scenic views.

*Accessibility:* Check for accessibility to transportation hubs, airports, or main roads for easier travel within the region.

## B. Amenities:

*Facilities Offered:* Assess the provided amenities like Wi-Fi availability, parking spaces, on-site dining options, laundry services, recreational facilities, or guided tours.

*Comfort Level:* Determine your comfort needs, whether you seek luxury amenities or prefer a simpler, more rustic experience.

## C. Budget:

*Price Range*: Alaska offers a wide range of accommodations catering to different budgets. Evaluate your budget constraints and match them with the available options, keeping in mind that prices may vary based on location and season.

## D. Seasonality:

*Peak Seasons:* Consider peak tourist seasons, especially during summer when the weather is more favorable, and wildlife sightings are common. Rates might be higher, and accommodations could get booked quickly during these times.

*Off-Season Travel:* Off-season travel may offer discounted rates and more availability, but weather conditions might be harsher in certain regions, especially during winter.

## E. Reviews and Ratings:

*Online Reviews:* Check reviews and ratings on reliable platforms like TripAdvisor, Google Reviews, or specific booking websites. Reading past guests' experiences can provide insights into the quality and service of the accommodations.

Recommendations: Seek recommendations from friends, family, or online travel communities for firsthand experiences and trusted suggestions.

By considering these factors, travelers can make informed decisions that align with their preferences and needs while ensuring a pleasant and satisfying stay in Alaska's diverse landscapes.

## Tips for Booking Accommodations

Alaska offers diverse accommodation options, and here are some tips for a smoother booking experience:

### A. Booking Websites:

Utilize Booking Platforms: Websites like Booking.com, Airbnb, or Expedia offer a wide range of accommodations. They provide filters for location, price range, amenities, and guest reviews, allowing you to compare and select the best-suited option.

### B. Direct Reservations:

Contact Accommodations Directly: Consider contacting accommodations directly via phone or email. This approach can sometimes yield better rates or offer additional insights into available amenities and services.

## C. Seasonal Reservations:

*Plan Early for Peak Seasons:* Alaska experiences peak seasons during summer for outdoor activities and festivals. Booking accommodations in advance, especially during June to August, ensures availability and better rates.

## D. Consideration of Special Offers:

*Check for Deals and Discounts:* Look for special packages, discounts, or promotional offers provided by accommodations. Sometimes, they offer exclusive deals on their websites or through newsletters, providing cost-effective stays.

Considering these tips while booking accommodations in Alaska can enhance your overall experience by ensuring a comfortable and suitable stay while also potentially saving on costs.

## Chapter Seven: Alaska Cuisine
### Local Alaskan Dishes to Try

Alaskan cuisine represents a fascinating blend of flavors and culinary traditions shaped by the state's diverse cultural influences and natural bounty. This rich tapestry of food culture weaves together Native Alaskan, Russian, and American culinary legacies, creating a unique and diverse gastronomic landscape that captivates locals and visitors alike.

Alaska's culinary heritage is deeply rooted in the practices of its Indigenous peoples, whose traditional diet includes a variety of foods sourced from the land, rivers, and seas. Native Alaskan cuisine reflects a profound connection to the natural environment, embracing ingredients like wild game meats, fish, berries, roots, and greens that sustained these communities for generations. Salmon, a cornerstone of Alaskan Indigenous diets, holds cultural significance and is prepared in myriad ways, from smoking and grilling to curing and baking.

Moreover, Alaskan Native cultures also celebrate unique delicacies like Eskimo ice cream, known as Akutaq, a traditional dessert made from whipped fat, berries, and sometimes fish. This indigenous dessert offers a sweet and creamy treat while highlighting the resourcefulness and adaptability of these cultures in using locally available ingredients.

The arrival of Russian explorers and settlers in the 18th century left an indelible mark on Alaskan cuisine. Russian influence introduced new ingredients and cooking techniques, such as hearty stews and soups like borscht, showcasing root vegetables and cabbage. The banya, a traditional Russian sauna, is linked to Alaskan cultural practices and is often followed by a meal featuring Russian-style dishes.

Subsequent American influence further diversified Alaskan cuisine. The Gold Rush era brought an influx of miners and settlers, leading to the introduction of American comfort foods and a fusion of culinary styles. This fusion resulted in a diverse culinary landscape that embraces American classics alongside traditional Alaskan fare.

## Fusion of Native, Russian, and American Influences in Alaskan Dishes

Alaskan cuisine is a beautiful mosaic reflecting the fusion of Native, Russian, and American culinary influences. This amalgamation is evident in various dishes that incorporate a blend of flavors and cooking techniques from these diverse cultural backgrounds.

Salmon remains an iconic Alaskan food, prepared in ways that blend Indigenous, Russian, and American influences. For instance, smoked salmon, a technique learned from Native Alaskans and further enhanced by Russian and American methods, produces a delicacy appreciated worldwide.

Russian influences are observed in dishes like solyanka, a hearty soup that features a medley of meats, pickles, and spices, reflecting a fusion of Slavic and Alaskan flavors. Additionally, pelmeni and dumplings filled with meat or fish showcase Russian culinary heritage while adapting to Alaskan ingredients like local game meats or seafood.

American influences have introduced classic comfort foods like burgers, sandwiches, and fried dishes to Alaskan cuisine. However, these American staples often take on an Alaskan twist, incorporating locally sourced ingredients like reindeer meat or wild berries, providing a unique and regional flavor profile.

This culinary fusion extends to desserts and beverages. While pies and pastries draw inspiration from American baking traditions, they may feature Alaskan berries like blueberries or cloudberries. Spruce tip beer, a distinctly Alaskan brew, embodies the fusion concept by blending indigenous ingredients with modern brewing techniques, creating a beer with citrusy and resinous notes.

In essence, Alaskan cuisine is a celebration of diversity, blending centuries-old Indigenous practices with influences from Russian settlers and American pioneers. This culinary fusion not only showcases the rich tapestry of cultural influences but also underscores the adaptability and resourcefulness of Alaskan food traditions in utilizing the region's abundant natural resources.

## Seafood Delicacies

### A. Wild Alaskan Salmon

Alaskan wild salmon, revered globally for its rich flavor and nutritional benefits, is a cornerstone of the state's cuisine. It comes in various species, such as king (chinook), sockeye (red), coho (silver), pink, and chum (keta), each offering unique tastes and textures. These salmon varieties are prepared using diverse cooking methods that highlight their natural flavors:

***a. Grilled Salmon:*** Grilling is a popular method that enhances the salmon's natural oils and smoky flavor. It's often seasoned with simple ingredients like salt, pepper, and herbs, allowing the salmon's taste to shine.

*b.* ***Smoked Salmon:*** Smoking salmon is a traditional preservation method, imparting a robust flavor. The process involves curing the fish with salt, sugar, and spices before smoking it over wood chips, creating tender, savory smoked salmon.

*c.* ***Baked Salmon:*** Baking salmon in the oven is a versatile and easy method. It can be baked with a variety of seasonings or sauces, such as lemon butter, maple glaze, or garlic herb, preserving its tenderness and juiciness.

*d.* ***Raw Salmon:*** Sushi lovers relish raw salmon in dishes like sashimi or nigiri. Fresh Alaskan salmon's exceptional quality makes it ideal for raw consumption, delivering a buttery texture and delicate taste.

## Best Places to Try Salmon-Based Dishes in Alaska:

**Ray's Waterfront:** Located in Seward, Ray's Waterfront offers delectable salmon dishes with a breathtaking view of Resurrection Bay. Their grilled salmon and smoked salmon chowder are highly recommended.

***The Saltry Restaurant:*** Situated in Halibut Cove, this rustic waterfront eatery specializes in local seafood, including innovative salmon preparations like cedar plank grilled salmon.

***The Crow's Nest:*** Anchorage's renowned restaurant atop Hotel Captain Cook offers fine dining with sweeping views of the city and serves exquisite baked salmon and salmon roulade.

These and many other eateries across Alaska take pride in serving a diverse range of salmon dishes, showcasing the state's bounty of premium wild-caught salmon in various culinary styles. Whether grilled, smoked, baked, or served raw, Alaskan salmon provides an exceptional dining experience that encapsulates the essence of the region's seafood.

## B. Halibut and Other Local Fish

**Signature Halibut Dishes:**

Alaskan halibut, known for its mild flavor and firm texture, is a sought-after delicacy in the region. Here are some signature halibut dishes:

*a. Halibut Tacos:* This dish features fresh halibut fillets grilled or fried and served in soft tortillas with toppings like cabbage slaw, avocado, salsa, and a zesty sauce, offering a delightful fusion of flavors and textures.

*b. Fish and Chips:* Alaskan fish and chips often use halibut, offering tender, flaky fillets coated in a crispy batter and paired with golden fries. The dish is commonly served with tartar sauce and lemon wedges.

*c. Pan-Seared Halibut:* Pan-seared halibut fillets seasoned with herbs and spices and cooked until golden brown on the outside while retaining its moistness within, providing a simple yet flavorful dish.

**Other Notable Alaskan Fish Varieties and Dishes:**

Besides halibut, Alaska boasts a diverse range of local fish species used in various delectable dishes:

*a. Black Cod (Sablefish):* Black cod, known for its rich, buttery taste, is often prepared with miso glaze and baked to perfection. The result is a succulent and flavorful dish that is highly popular in Alaskan restaurants.

*b. Rockfish:* Alaskan rockfish is a versatile fish used in various preparations, including grilled rockfish fillets seasoned with local herbs, pan-seared rockfish tacos, or rockfish chowder made with fresh vegetables and broth.

*c. Arctic Char:* This cold-water fish resembling salmon in appearance and taste is often served grilled or smoked, offering a unique flavor profile and tender texture.

*d. Lingcod:* Lingcod, another prized Alaskan fish, is celebrated for its firm texture and mild flavor. It's commonly used in dishes such as lingcod fish tacos or lingcod fillets cooked with garlic butter.

*e. Salmon and Cod Varieties:* Apart from halibut, Alaskan cuisine features various salmon (king, sockeye, coho, etc.) and cod preparations, including grilled salmon steaks, cod fillets in creamy sauces, and salmon burgers.

These fish varieties are celebrated for their freshness and are frequently showcased in Alaskan cuisine. Restaurants and eaties across the state proudly incorporate these local fish into their menus, providing visitors and locals alike with a diverse array of delicious seafood options.

## Reindeer Sausage

*Description of Reindeer Sausage:*

Reindeer sausage is a traditional Alaskan specialty crafted from lean reindeer meat combined with various seasonings like garlic, pepper, and other spices. This sausage is often encased in natural casings and can be smoked or cooked by grilling, frying, or boiling. The taste is savory, with a slightly gamey flavor and a tender, juicy texture.

Traditional preparation methods involve grinding the lean reindeer meat along with a mix of herbs and spices, shaping the mixture into sausage links, and then smoking or cooking them slowly until they reach a deliciously aromatic and flavorful state.

## Recommended Restaurants or Markets Offering Reindeer Sausage:

*Alaska Sausage & Seafood (Anchorage, AK):* This renowned market offers various types of sausages, including reindeer sausage, known for their quality and flavor.

*Rust's Flying Service (Anchorage, AK):* The Rust's Market offers a selection of local Alaskan meats, including reindeer sausage, perfect for picnics or flights across the state.

*Fairbanks Alaska Public Market:* This market often hosts vendors selling reindeer sausage and other Alaskan delicacies made from local meats.

## Wild Game Dishes

Alaskan cuisine features an array of wild game meats such as caribou, moose, and bear. These meats are considered traditional sources of protein and have been part of Indigenous diets for centuries.

### Notable Dishes Featuring Wild Game Meats:

*Caribou Stew:* Caribou meat, known for its lean and rich flavor, is often used in hearty stews with root vegetables and herbs, slow-cooked to tender perfection.

*Moose Steak:* Moose meat, characterized by its robust flavor and tenderness, is served as steaks or cutlets, sometimes marinated and grilled or pan-seared to medium-rare for optimal taste.

*Bear Chili:* Bear meat, when properly handled and cooked, can be used in various recipes. Bear chili is one such dish where the meat is slow-cooked with beans, tomatoes, and spices, creating a hearty and flavorful meal.

It's important to note that these wild game meats are typically sourced by hunters and are not commonly found in restaurants due to regulatory restrictions. However, some specialized restaurants and local markets may occasionally offer dishes featuring these meats, providing a unique culinary experience for adventurous food enthusiasts in Alaska.

## Eskimo Ice Cream (Akutaq)

Akutaq, also known as Eskimo ice cream, is a traditional dessert crafted by Alaska Natives. The dish combines locally sourced ingredients, primarily whipped fat (traditionally animal fat such as seal or reindeer), along with berries like blueberries, cranberries, cloudberries, or salmonberries. Sometimes, sugar, honey, or other sweeteners are added for taste. This mixture is whipped together until it achieves a creamy, pudding-like consistency.

### Where to Find and Sample Akutaq in Alaska:

Sampling Akutaq can be a unique experience often found in cultural events, festivals, or specific Indigenous gatherings. Sometimes, restaurants specializing in Indigenous cuisine or cultural centers in Alaska may offer this traditional dessert. Additionally, visitors might encounter Akutaq demonstrations or tastings during cultural exhibits or community events.

## Other Native Foods

*Fry Bread:* A staple in Indigenous cultures, fry bread is a flatbread made from dough that is deep-fried until it puffs up, creating a crispy exterior and a soft inside. It's often served as a base for various dishes or with sweet toppings like honey or powdered sugar.

*Smoked Salmon:* Indigenous communities have been smoking salmon for centuries. Salmon fillets are cured and then smoked over wood, resulting in a flavorful and preserved fish with a distinctive taste.

### Cultural Significance and Availability of These Dishes:

These dishes hold immense cultural significance for Indigenous communities, passed down through generations as part of their heritage and traditional culinary practices. While they might not always be readily available in commercial restaurants, visitors can sometimes find these foods at cultural events, Native-owned eateries, or local markets that celebrate and promote Indigenous Alaskan cuisine. Some restaurants and food establishments have also begun incorporating these traditional dishes into their menus, acknowledging their cultural importance and offering visitors a taste of authentic Indigenous Alaskan foods.

# Berry-Based Desserts

## Alaskan Berries and Their Use in Desserts:

Alaska is abundant in a variety of wild berries like blueberries, salmonberries, lingonberries, and cloudberries. These berries find their way into various desserts due to their rich flavors and local availability. Blueberries, with their sweet-tart taste, and salmonberries, known for their bright, slightly tart flavor, are commonly used in desserts like pies, jams, and cobblers.

### Berry-Based Desserts Commonly Found in Alaska:

*Berry Cobbler:* A classic dessert made with a mix of locally foraged berries topped with a sweet, biscuit-like crust.

*Berry Jams and Preserves:* Locally made jams and preserves often feature a variety of berries, perfect for spreading on bread or pairing with pastries.

*Berry Tarts:* These tarts showcase the vibrant colors and flavors of Alaskan berries in a delightful pastry crust, often topped with whipped cream or served with ice cream.

## Frontier-Style Pies and Pastries

Frontier-style pies and pastries in Alaska reflect a rustic and hearty approach to baking. These treats often embody the spirit of homesteaders and pioneer cooking, focusing on simple yet satisfying recipes using locally sourced ingredients. Pies made with rhubarb, berries, or even savory fillings like salmon or reindeer are notable examples.

## Recommended Bakeries or Cafes to Try These Sweet Treats:

*The Kobuk Coffee Co.* (Anchorage): Offers a selection of pies and pastries, including berry pies made with Alaskan-grown berries.

*The Runcible Spoon Bakery (Homer):* Known for its assortment of frontier-style pies, tarts, and pastries showcasing local flavors and ingredients.

*Fire Island Rustic Bakeshop (Anchorage):* Offers a variety of baked goods made from scratch, often featuring seasonal berries in their desserts.

These desserts and sweets celebrate the bounty of Alaskan berries and the heritage of frontier-style baking, offering a taste of the region's culinary traditions with each delightful bite.

## List of recommended eateries and restaurants in Alaska:

### 1. Simon & Seafort's

**Location:** 420 L St, Anchorage, AK 99501, United States

Phone: +1 907-274-3502

**Website:** simonandseaforts.com

**Overview:** Known for seafood & steaks with a dining room offering views.

**Services:** Private dining room, great cocktails, Wi-Fi.

## 2. Seven Glaciers Restaurant

**Location:** 1000 Arlberg Ave, Girdwood, AK 99587, United States

**Phone:** +1 907-754-2237

**Website:** alyeskaresort.com

**Overview:** Fine dining with scenic views in Girdwood.

**Services:** Reservations are required, vegetarian dishes and high chairs are available.

## 3. The Saltry Restaurant

**Location:** 1 West Ismailof, Halibut Cove, AK 99603, United States

**Phone:** +1 907-226-2424

**Website:** thesaltryrestaurant.com

**Overview:** A seafood restaurant offering picturesque views.

### 4. Marx Bros. Cafe

**Location:** 627 W 3rd Ave, Anchorage, AK 99501, United States

**Phone:** +1 907-278-2133

**Website:** places.singleplatform.com

**Overview:** Anchorage eatery specializing in fresh seafood and creative dishes.

**Services:** Reservations required, fireplace.

### 5. Crush Wine Bistro & Cellar

**Location:** 328 G St, Anchorage, AK 99501, United States

**Phone:** +1 907-865-9198

**Website:** crushak.com

**Overview:** Known for wine selection and contemporary American dishes.

**Services:** Outdoor seating.

### 6. Double Musky Inn

**Location:** Mile, 3 Crow Creek Rd, Girdwood, AK 99587, United States

**Phone:** +1 907-783-2822

**Website:** doublemuskyinn.com

**Overview:** Cajun-inspired cuisine in Girdwood.

## 7. *Snow City Cafe*

**Location:** 1034 W 4th Ave, Anchorage, AK 99501, United States

**Phone:** +1 907-272-2489

**Website:** snowcitycafe.com

**Overview:** A popular breakfast spot in Anchorage.

## 8. *The Bake Shop*

**Location:** 194 Olympic Mountain Loop, Girdwood, AK 99587, United States

**Phone:** +1 907-783-2831

**Website:** thebakeshop.com

**Overview:** Talkeetna cafe is known for pastries and sandwiches.

## 9. F Street Station

**Location:** 325 F St, Anchorage, AK 99501, United States

**Phone:** +1 907-272-5196

**Overview:** Anchorage restaurant offering Alaskan seafood.

**Services:** Serves great cocktails, no reservations.

### 10. Orso

**Location:** 737 W 5th Ave #110, Anchorage, AK 99501, United States

**Phone:** +1 907-222-3232

**Website:** orsoalaska.com

**Overview**: Downtown Anchorage restaurant serving contemporary American cuisine.

**Services:** Fireplace, private dining room, vegetarian dishes.

### 11. The Cookery

**Location:** 209 5th Ave, Seward, AK 99664, United States

**Phone:** +1 907-422-7459

**Website:** cookeryseward.com

**Overview:** Seward restaurant focuses on locally sourced ingredients.

**Services:** Serves vegetarian dishes; high chairs available.

### 12. Ray's Waterfront

**Location:** 1316 4th Ave, Seward, AK 99664, United States

**Phone:** +1 907-224-5606

**Website:** rayswaterfront.com

**Overview:** Seafood restaurant in Seward with scenic views of Resurrection Bay.

## Summary of the Diverse and Unique Culinary Offerings in Alaska:

Alaska's culinary landscape is a rich tapestry woven from a blend of indigenous, frontier, and modern influences. The state's cuisine is renowned for its variety, featuring an array of seafood delicacies, game meats, indigenous dishes, and locally sourced ingredients. Berries like blueberries and salmonberries, game meats such as reindeer sausage, and seafood like wild Alaskan salmon are emblematic ingredients that find their way into Alaskan recipes, showcasing the region's rich natural bounty.

The fusion of Native, Russian, and American culinary traditions contributes to a vibrant gastronomic scene, evident in the hearty frontier-style pies, intricate berry-based desserts, and the distinctive flavors of locally brewed craft beers. Alaskan cuisine not only nourishes the body but also serves as a gateway to understanding the state's history, culture, and connection to its pristine natural surroundings.

For travelers visiting Alaska, delving into the local cuisine is an integral part of experiencing the state's culture. Exploring the culinary delights of Alaska offers a unique opportunity to connect with the land, its people, and their customs. Whether savoring freshly caught seafood, tasting indigenous dishes, or enjoying frontier-style pies made with wild berries, embracing Alaskan cuisine promises an enriching and flavorful journey.

Embrace the chance to visit local bakeries, seafood shacks, and restaurants that showcase the diverse flavors of the region. Engage with locals, indulge in the varied culinary offerings, and relish the distinctive tastes that reflect Alaska's heritage and natural abundance. By immersing in the flavors of Alaska, travelers can create lasting memories while appreciating the culinary heritage deeply rooted in this magnificent northern state.

# Chapter Eight: Hiking and Trekking

## Hiking and Trekking Trails in Alaska

Alaska's diverse landscape offers some of the most captivating and challenging hiking and trekking trails in the world. From its rugged mountains to its expansive forests and stunning coastlines, the state provides an array of options for adventurers seeking unforgettable experiences amidst raw, untamed nature.

Alaska boasts an extensive network of trails catering to all skill levels, from leisurely day hikes to demanding multi-day treks. Denali National Park, home to North America's highest peak, Mount Denali, offers trails like the Triple Lakes Trail and Savage Alpine Trail, providing stunning views of the park's diverse terrain. Another iconic spot is the Chugach State Park, just outside Anchorage, offering trails like the Crow Pass Trail, leading through dense forests and alpine meadows.

**Activities and Attractions:**

Visitors can explore Glacier Bay National Park's trails, such as the Bartlett River Trail, winding through lush rainforests, or head to the Tongass National Forest for the West Glacier Trail. For the experienced hiker, the Resurrection Pass Trail near Hope challenges with breathtaking views of Resurrection Bay. Those seeking unique experiences might consider the Historic Iditarod Trail, tracing the route of the famous sled dog race.

**Tips and Recommendations:**

It's crucial to prepare adequately before embarking on a hike in Alaska. Check weather conditions, carry essential gear, bear deterrents, and ensure physical fitness. Some trails require permits, so verify regulations beforehand. During the summer, trails are more accessible, but bear sightings may increase; therefore, being bear-aware is essential.

# Wildlife Watching in Alaska

Alaska is a wildlife enthusiast's paradise, renowned for its diverse ecosystems and abundant wildlife. From majestic marine creatures to iconic land mammals and impressive avian species, the state offers unparalleled opportunities for wildlife observation in their natural habitats.

Alaska's wildlife can be found across various regions, each offering unique species and habitats. The Kenai Fjords National Park and Prince William Sound provide exceptional marine wildlife encounters, including humpback whales, orcas, sea otters, and puffins. Denali National Park is home to grizzly bears, moose, caribou, Dall sheep, and wolves, making it a must-visit for terrestrial wildlife enthusiasts.

**Activities and Attractions:**

Visitors can embark on guided tours, cruises, or self-guided hikes to observe wildlife. The Kodiak National Wildlife Refuge is renowned for its Kodiak bears, while the Arctic

National Wildlife Refuge offers glimpses of polar bears, muskoxen, and migratory birds. The McNeil River State Game Sanctuary provides unique opportunities to observe brown bears in their natural habitat.

**Tips and Recommendations:**

Respect wildlife and maintain a safe distance. Binoculars, cameras, and field guides are essential for a rewarding experience. Plan visits during specific seasons for increased chances of wildlife sightings, such as spring for bears emerging from hibernation or summer for marine wildlife activities.

**Conservation and Respect:**

It's critical to adhere to ethical wildlife viewing practices to minimize disturbance to animals and their habitats. Following Leave No Trace principles and respecting designated wildlife sanctuaries and regulations are vital.

## Fishing and Hunting in Alaska

Alaska is a haven for outdoor enthusiasts, offering world-class fishing and hunting experiences. Its pristine rivers, abundant lakes, and vast wilderness provide exceptional opportunities for anglers and hunters to engage in their favorite pursuits.

Alaska boasts an array of fish species, including salmon, trout, char, halibut, and more. The state's rivers and streams are teeming with prized catches like king salmon, silver salmon, and rainbow trout. The Kenai River, Bristol Bay, and the Russian River are renowned for salmon runs, attracting anglers from across the globe.

Hunting in Alaska is a cherished tradition and offers opportunities for big game, including moose, caribou, Dall sheep, and brown and black bears. Different regions offer varied hunting experiences, such as moose hunting in the Kenai Peninsula or brown bear hunting in Kodiak Island.

### Activities and Attractions:

Fishing enthusiasts can enjoy fly fishing, deep-sea fishing, and ice fishing, depending on the season and location. Many charter companies and lodges offer guided fishing trips with expert local guides. Guided tours and outfitters provide expertise and assistance for a successful and ethical hunting experience.

### Regulations and Safety:

Both fishing and hunting require adherence to state regulations and licensing. Understanding bag limits, seasons, and specific regulations for each species is crucial. Safety measures, including bear safety protocols during hunting trips, are imperative.

### Conservation and Ethics:

Alaska emphasizes conservation ethics in fishing and hunting. It's vital to follow catch-and-release practices, respect bag limits, and participate in sustainable and responsible hunting practices to preserve the state's wildlife and ecosystems.

# Winter Sports and Northern Lights Viewing

Alaska's winter season presents a playground for winter sports enthusiasts and an opportunity to witness the breathtaking Northern Lights. From skiing down powdery slopes to witnessing the aurora borealis dance across the night sky, Alaska offers an array of thrilling experiences.

Alaska's winter sports scene includes skiing, snowboarding, snowmobiling, dog mushing, ice fishing, and more. Alyeska Resort in Girdwood and Arctic Valley Ski Area in Anchorage are popular destinations for downhill skiing and snowboarding. Snowmobile trails traverse vast terrains, providing thrilling adventures through snowy landscapes.

Dog sledding tours offer a unique experience, allowing visitors to ride along with sled dogs through the wilderness.

Alaska's vastness and location within the auroral oval make it a prime spot for witnessing the mesmerizing Northern Lights. Fairbanks, Anchorage, and the Denali region are among the best places to see the aurora. The winter months, particularly from September to April, offer the best chances to witness this natural phenomenon.

**Activities and Attractions:**

Winter sports enthusiasts can explore various terrains for skiing, snowboarding, and snowmobiling. Dog sledding tours let visitors experience the thrill of mushing through snowy trails. Ice fishing on frozen lakes and rivers is a popular pastime during winter.

**Northern Lights Activities:**

Travelers can embark on guided aurora tours that take them to optimal viewing locations away from city lights. Tours often include informative sessions on the aurora and provide the best chances to witness the dancing lights. Visitors can also opt to stay in lodges or cabins with Northern Lights viewing options.

**Precautions and Planning:**

When engaging in winter sports, proper gear, including warm clothing and safety equipment, is essential. For Northern Lights viewing, choose locations with minimal light pollution and be prepared for long periods outdoors in cold weather.

## Chapter Nine: Practical Tips for Exploring Alaska

**Practical Tips for Exploring Alaska:** Navigating the Last Frontier

Alaska, with its stunning landscapes and untamed wilderness, beckons an increasing number of intrepid travelers each year. The Last Frontier, as it's aptly called, presents unique challenges and awe-inspiring experiences. As you gear up for your Alaskan adventure, arm yourself with practical tips to ensure a safe, budget-friendly, and truly fulfilling exploration.

# Safety Guidelines

## 1. Safety Guidelines: Navigating Alaska's Wilderness

Alaska's wilderness is breathtaking, but it comes with its own set of challenges. Wildlife encounters are not uncommon, underscoring the need for heightened wildlife awareness. Whether you're hiking, camping, or exploring, always carry bear spray, make noise to alert wildlife, and educate yourself on their habits to foster a harmonious coexistence.

Weather in Alaska is famously unpredictable, contributing to potential accidents. To stay safe, dress in layers, pack rain gear and stay updated on weather forecasts. Inform someone about your travel plans, especially if you're venturing into remote areas, and consider the expertise of a local guide.

Navigating the vast and sometimes confusing terrain of Alaska requires preparation. Ensure you have essential tools like GPS, paper maps, and a satellite phone for emergencies. Familiarize yourself with the landscape beforehand and plan your routes meticulously.

Water safety is paramount in a state adorned with beautiful water bodies. Incidents related to water activities are not uncommon, emphasizing the importance of wearing a life jacket and being mindful of changing conditions, such as tides and currents.

Health precautions are essential due to Alaska's remote nature. Carry a basic first aid kit, necessary medications, and secure travel insurance with evacuation coverage to address any unforeseen medical emergencies.

## Money-Saving Tips

### 2. Money-Saving Tips: Maximizing Your Alaskan Adventure

Exploring Alaska during the off-peak season can significantly cut costs, offering more affordable accommodation, tours, and transportation options. Embrace the tranquility of Alaska with fewer crowds while enjoying financial savings.

Alaska's culinary scene is a delightful surprise, and opting for local eateries proves not only a budget-friendly choice but also an opportunity to savor authentic Alaskan flavors. Dine like a local and discover the diverse culinary offerings.

Camping in the vast Alaskan wilderness provides a cost-effective alternative to traditional accommodation. Thoughtful site selection, adhering to Leave No Trace principles, ensures a budget-friendly and environmentally conscious stay.

Public transportation, such as buses and ferries, can be more economical than renting a car, especially in remote areas. Save on transportation costs while taking in the scenic beauty of Alaska.

Package deals for tours and accommodations are prevalent, offering substantial savings. Research and plan your itinerary to take advantage of bundled activities, providing both convenience and financial benefits.

## Communication and Connectivity

### 3. Communication and Connectivity: Staying Connected in the Wilderness

While cellular coverage may be limited in certain wilderness areas, major towns and cities generally have reliable networks. Consider purchasing a local SIM card for better rates and connectivity during your travels.

In more remote areas, satellite phones prove invaluable for reliable communication in emergencies. Renting one for short-term use ensures a lifeline to the outside world in areas with limited connectivity.

Wi-Fi may be sparse, especially in rural areas, so plan accordingly. Utilize offline maps and apps for navigation, allowing you to explore even in locations with limited internet access.

Maintain a list of essential contacts, including local emergency services, embassy details, and those of your travel companions. Sharing your itinerary with someone trustworthy adds an extra layer of safety to your journey.

## Sustainable Tourism Practices

**4. Sustainable Tourism Practices: Preserving Alaska's Beauty**

Adhering to Leave No Trace principles is crucial for preserving Alaska's pristine beauty. Ensure you pack out all waste, stay on designated trails, and respect wildlife habitats to minimize your environmental impact.

Support local initiatives and businesses to contribute to the local economy while fostering sustainable tourism practices. Alaska is home to a thriving community of artisans and entrepreneurs waiting to be discovered.

Consider ecotourism options that prioritize environmental conservation and responsible tourism practices. Choose tours and activities that align with your commitment to preserving Alaska's unique ecosystems.

Educate yourself about the local environment, wildlife, and cultural norms. A deeper understanding not only enhances your experience but also promotes responsible and sustainable travel practices.

These practical tips will serve as your compass through the rugged beauty of Alaska. By prioritizing safety, embracing budget-friendly strategies, ensuring effective communication, and adopting sustainable tourism practices, you're not only enhancing your personal adventure but contributing to the preservation of Alaska's natural wonders for generations to come.

# Contact Information for Travelers

Navigating a new destination, especially one as vast and diverse as Alaska, requires having essential contact information readily available. Whether you encounter an emergency, need local assistance, or simply seek information, having the right contacts can make your journey more secure and enjoyable.

Here's an extensive guide to contact information for travelers in Alaska:

## Emergency Services

- **Police Emergency:** Dial 911
- In case of emergencies requiring police intervention.

- **Medical Emergency:** Dial 911 for immediate medical assistance and ambulance services.

- **Fire Emergency:** Dial 911 for fire-related emergencies.

## Health Services

- **Alaska Regional Hospital:**
- Address: 2801 Debarr Road, Anchorage, AK
- Phone: +1 907-276-1131

- **Providence Alaska Medical Center:**
- Address: 3200 Providence Drive, Anchorage, AK
- Phone: +1 907-562-2211

## Embassy and Consulate Information

- **U.S. Embassy in Anchorage:**
- Address: 3601 C Street, Suite 1300, Anchorage, AK
- Phone: +1 907-272-1484

- **Website: U.S. Embassy in Anchorage**
- Canadian Consulate in Anchorage:
- Address: 1029 W. 3rd Avenue, Suite 201, Anchorage, AK
- Phone: +1 907-278-5719
- Website: Canadian Consulate in Anchorage

# Transportation Services

- **Alaska Railroad Corporation:**
- Phone: +1 800-544-0552
- Website: Alaska Railroad: https://www.alaskarailroad.com/
- **Alaska Marine Highway System (Ferries):**
- Phone: +1 800-642-0066
- Website: Alaska Marine Highway

- **Ted Stevens Anchorage International Airport:**
- Phone: +1 907-266-2526
- Website: Ted Stevens Anchorage

- **International Airport:**
  https://www.tedstevensanchorageinternationalairport.com/

## Tourism and Visitor Centers:

- **Alaska Travel Industry Association:**
- Phone: +1 907-929-2842
- Website: AlaskaTIA:
  https://www.alaskatia.org/

- **Alaska Public Lands Information Centers:**
- Website: Alaska Centers:
  https://www.alaskacenters.gov/

## Local Utilities

- **Emergency Roadside Assistance (AAA):**
- Phone: 1-800-AAA-HELP

- **Alaska Gas Utility:**
- Phone: +1 907-458-8452

- **Chugach Electric Association:**
- Phone: +1 907-563-7494

## Outdoor Emergency Services

- **Alaska State Troopers Search and Rescue:**
- Phone (Search and Rescue Coordination): +1 907-451-5100
-
- **Alaska Mountain Rescue Group:**
- Phone (Non-Emergency): +1 907-783-0690

- **Wildlife and Park Information:**
- Alaska Department of Fish and Game:
- Phone: +1 907-267-2257
- Website: ADF&G


- **Denali National Park Visitor Center:**
- Phone: +1 907-683-9532
- Website: Denali National Park


## Communication Services

- **Alaska Communications:**
- Phone: +1 800-808-8083
- Website: Alaska Communications: https://www.alaskacommunications.com/

- **GCI (General Communication Inc.):**

- Phone: +1 800-800-4800
- Website: GCI: https://www.gci.com/

## Local Tourism Boards

- **Alaska Tourism Marketing Board:**
- Phone: +1 907-929-2842
- Website: AlaskaTIA:
  https://www.alaskatia.org/

- **Visit Anchorage:**
- Phone: +1 907-276-4118
- Website: Visit Anchorage:
- https://www.anchorage.net/

Make sure to save these contact details, and consider having a physical copy and digital backup for easy access during your travels in Alaska. Safe travels!

## Conclusion

As you reach the culmination of this Alaskan travel guide, your anticipation is undoubtedly brimming with the promise of adventure, exploration, and the unrivaled beauty that awaits in the Last Frontier. Alaska, with its majestic landscapes, unique wildlife, and diverse cultures, is more than a destination—it's an immersive journey into the heart of nature's grandeur. Let's take a moment to reflect on the insights shared, encourage your spirit of discovery, and offer additional tips to ensure your Alaskan experience is nothing short of extraordinary.

## A Recap of Your Alaskan Adventure:

Your journey through this guide has been a virtual expedition across the vast expanse of Alaska, touching on essential aspects that will enhance your travel experience. From safety guidelines for navigating the wilderness to money-saving tips allowing you to explore on a budget, communication insights ensuring connectivity in remote areas, and sustainable tourism practices to preserve Alaska's pristine beauty—each section has been meticulously crafted to serve as your compass through the rugged and enchanting terrain.

Safety-conscious travelers will find valuable tips on wildlife awareness, weather preparedness, navigation tools, water safety, and health precautions. These insights, rooted in both statistical data and seasoned wisdom, are designed to empower you to explore with confidence and mindfulness.

For those seeking a budget-friendly adventure, the guide unveils the secrets of off-peak travel, local culinary delights, camping options, public transportation alternatives, and the

217

allure of package deals. Embrace these strategies, and you'll not only save money but also immerse yourself in the authentic Alaskan experience that lies beyond the tourist hotspots.

Communication and connectivity are essential in Alaska's remote expanses. Whether you're staying connected with loved ones or navigating the wilderness, the guide provides information on cellular coverage, satellite communication, internet access, and emergency contacts to keep you informed and secure.

In the realm of sustainable tourism practices, you've been introduced to the principles of Leave No Trace, the significance of supporting local initiatives, and the growing popularity of ecotourism in Alaska. By adopting these practices, you become a steward of the environment, ensuring that future generations can revel in the unspoiled beauty of this pristine land.

**Encouragement for Your Alaskan Exploration:**

As you stand at the threshold of your Alaskan adventure, let the spirit of discovery and wonder propel you forward. Alaska is not just a destination; it's an opportunity to connect with nature in its purest form, to witness wildlife in their natural habitats, and to experience the untamed beauty that has inspired generations of explorers.

**Embrace the Unexpected:**

Alaska is a land of surprises, where nature unfolds its wonders in unexpected ways. Be open to spontaneous detours, hidden trails, and chance encounters. Some of the most memorable experiences lie beyond the well-trodden paths, waiting to be discovered by those with a sense of curiosity and adventure.

**Immerse Yourself in Local Culture:**

Beyond its breathtaking landscapes, Alaska is home to diverse cultures and communities. Take the time to engage with locals, learn about their traditions, and savor the rich tapestry of Alaskan heritage. Attend cultural events, visit museums, and let the stories of the people become an integral part of your Alaskan narrative.

**Capture the Moments:**

Alaska's beauty is fleeting, with the dance of the Northern Lights, the fleeting visits of wildlife, and the ever-changing landscapes. Arm yourself with a camera, whether it's a professional DSLR or a smartphone, and capture the moments that will etch themselves into your memory. Each snapshot is a testament to the raw and unfiltered allure of the Last Frontier.

**Respect and Preserve:**

As you traverse this pristine wilderness, remember that you are a guest in a delicate ecosystem. Follow Leave No Trace principles religiously, respect wildlife habitats, and leave the landscapes as untouched as you found them. Your responsible actions today contribute to the preservation of Alaska's untouched beauty for future generations.

## Additional Tips for a Deeper Understanding of Alaska:

### *1. Read Alaskan Literature:*

Enhance your understanding of Alaska's soul by delving into literature inspired by this vast land. Works like "Into the Wild" by Jon Krakauer, "The Call of the Wild" by Jack London, and "Coming into the Country" by John McPhee offer profound insights into the spirit of Alaska.

### *2. Attend Local Events:*

Check local event calendars for festivals, fairs, and gatherings that celebrate Alaskan culture. From native dances to dog mushing competitions, participating in these events provides a firsthand look into the vibrant traditions that shape the state.

### *3. Take a Scenic Flight:*

To truly grasp the immensity and grandeur of Alaska, consider taking a scenic flight. Witnessing the vast landscapes, towering mountains, and sprawling glaciers from above provides a perspective that is both humbling and awe-inspiring.

### *4. Learn Basic Wilderness Skills:*

Equip yourself with basic wilderness skills to enhance your confidence in the great outdoors. Understanding basic navigation, survival techniques, and outdoor safety will not only add a layer of preparedness but also deepen your connection with the wilderness.

### *5. Embrace the Midnight Sun:*

If your travels align with the summer months, embrace the phenomenon of the Midnight Sun. Experience the surreal beauty of a sun that never truly sets, casting an ethereal glow on the landscapes. It's a unique Alaskan spectacle that captivates the senses.

As you embark on this Alaskan odyssey, may your senses be awakened by the untamed beauty, may your spirit be fueled by the sense of adventure, and may your journey be etched into the annals of your most cherished memories. Alaska awaits, with its rugged landscapes, thriving wildlife, and a spirit of exploration that transcends time. Safe travels, intrepid adventurer, as you venture into the heart of the Last Frontier!

Made in the USA
Coppell, TX
02 February 2024

28491230R00125